Fighting to Find
G O D

Fighting to Find
G O D

Eric Wahlin

Copyright © 2018 by Eric Wahlin
All rights reserved, including the right to reproduce this book, or portions thereof, in any form. No part of this book may be used or reproduced in any manner whatsoever without written permission from the author, except in the case of brief quotations embodied in critical articles and reviews. The views expressed herein are the responsibility of the author and do not necessarily represent the position of the publisher. For information or permission, write: ericwahlin@gmail.com.

This is a work of creative nonfiction. The events herein are portrayed to the best of the author's memory. While all the stories in this book are true, some names and identifying details may have been changed to protect the privacy of the people involved.

Cover photo credit: Amanda Lynn
Editorial work and production management by Eschler Editing
Cover design by Jason Robinson
Interior print design and layout by Marny K. Parkin
Published by Scrivener Books

ISBN 978-0-9986254-9-2
First Edition: August 2018
Printed in the United States of America
10 9 8 7 6 5 4 3 2 1

Contents

Acknowledgments — vii

Chapter 1
Questions — 1

Chapter 2
What Is the Best Martial Art? — 7

Chapter 3
Finding God — 13

Chapter 4
Fundamentals — 31

Chapter 5
Spiritual and Physical Growth — 41

Chapter 6
Fight Principles — 49

Chapter 7
How Does Your Corner Affect the Fight? — 59

Chapter 8
The Importance of Structure in Finding God — 79

Chapter 9
Fighting with Your Eternal Family and Fighting for Your Eternal Family — 97

Chapter 10
Your Greatest Weapon   105

Bonus Material
Developing Structure to Achieve Your Fighting Goals   141

About the Author   161

Note to the Reader   163

Acknowledgments

I WOULD LIKE TO THANK KAREN, my wife, as she has been a huge support in my writing of this book. She has always supported me in my business, my fighting, and church callings. It is very apparent that without her this book would have never been possible. I would also like to thank my children, Grant and Grace, and the many life lessons I've learned from being their father. Another thanks goes out to Phil, my business partner, who has always been patient, easy to work with, and is the foundation of Factum MMA. I would also like to thank Tim, my boxing coach, who has for years been reliable and hardworking and has inspired me to become the best fighter I could possibly be. And, lastly, I want to thank all of my teammates at Factum—those who have been there in the early morning training sessions, out-of-town competitions, for the late-night conversations, for those who have punched me in the face and who have let me punch them in the face and made my dream job possible.

Chapter 1
Questions

I AM A MIXED MARTIAL ARTS fighter—and a Mormon. Not a common combination, for sure, but it's one that has actually led me to find God and the happiness that comes with truly knowing Him and having a relationship with Him. Have you ever wondered:

Is there a God?

Who is God?

Where did I come from?

Where am I going?

Can I prove there is a God?

What does God expect of me?

How will God communicate with me?

There was a time when I wondered about the answers to these questions. I have always gone to church, and so you may think my answers came from church. That's partially true. The *answers* did come from church. But that's it—they were just answers. They were not a convincing, undeniable, soul-satisfying truth; they simply satisfied a question—but not me. I still felt empty. I was not sure the answers I'd received were *true*. My church, like most churches, had the answers to these questions, but I still had to fight to find God. I hope to explore with you not only how you can receive the answers to these questions but how you can know whether or not they are true.

Let me ask these questions again, then answer them with the typical Sunday school answers I was given:

Is there a God? Yes.

Who is God? He is an all-powerful being.

Where did I come from? I dwelt with God in a spiritual existence before I was born.

Where am I going? When I die, my spirit will go to the spirit world and be prepared to receive a perfect, resurrected body. Then, through the Atonement of Christ, my spirit will be cleansed so I will be qualified to dwell with God in heaven forever.

Can I prove there is a God? No, but the key lies in having faith.

What does God expect of me? He expects me to live a good life, work hard, and serve others.

How will God communicate with me? Through the Holy Ghost and the scriptures.

There is a big difference between knowing the answers and *knowing* the answers. The lessons I learned from fighting became valuable and took me from not just knowing the church answers but to knowing God personally. This book explains how I used fight principles to discover and come to know God.

One fight concept I used in my quest to find God was trial and error. It is through trial and error that a fighter develops, and it is through trial and error that we create a relationship with God. On the cover of this book is a picture of me getting kicked in the head. I chose that picture because I really grew as a fighter after that particular fight. Obviously, my game plan and technique were off—that kick to the head was the blow that finished me. After that, I had to go back to the drawing board and work hard to correct my mistakes and develop better muscle memory. I had to lose a fight to become a better fighter. Discovering God is a similar process. If you want to find God, you must admit when you are wrong and allow God to break you down so He can build you into something stronger.

The best fighters are willing to put themselves out there, compete often, and accept losing as a learning experience. I have seen fighters do all sorts of crazy things to avoid losing. Most common is skipping out on sparring class. It's not fun getting beat up in front of your friends. One excuse I often hear is "Sorry, I can't spar today. I forgot my mouthpiece." I've heard just about every excuse in the book, on all levels, whether from young kids trying to avoid sparring or professional champions ducking a number-one contender. The fact is, losing a fight is awful, but it is in those dark, lonely moments after a loss that a champion gets up and works hard to ensure victory over their next opponent.

A simple truth I've discovered is that it's okay to lose a fight. It's also okay to misunderstand God. The correlation between losing a fight and not correctly understanding God is that both hurt either physically or emotionally. Losing a fight upsets me because I look at fighting as if it were a life-or-death situation. When I lose a fight, I assume I would have died if it were a fight to the death. That may seem over the top, but I believe some people are born with a battle mentality; they need physical conflict in their lives so they can bring value to their existence through combat. Why is a battle mentality important? Some may see it as a violent and barbaric attribute, but it can also be seen as loving and protective. No one likes the thought of their loved ones being hurt, and fighting helps fill that void. It makes sense that if you can fight, you can protect. I feel it is my responsibility in life to protect the ones I love. And when I lose a fight, I start to wonder if I have what it takes to save my life and protect my family in a life-or-death situation.

Likewise, not understanding God is a life-or-death situation. It means you do not understand your destination in the afterlife. With that destination unsure, you are faced with the fact you may cease to exist after you die or be sentenced to hell, or damned. Our progression being damned can come in many different ways. We may understand our religion yet feel unsure whether or not we believe it, thus our postmortal destination is unsure. Or, we may want a religion but are not sure which one is true; not having a belief system would mean you don't have a defined afterlife or the information required to qualify for postmortal paradise. Others may struggle with the fact that they simply do not believe in God, which means they are faced with total death at the end of their mortal journey. I say total death because if there is no God, there is no existence after this life.

Within these examples we see several different mind-sets. Some believe in God yet do not understand God, which sentences them to an afterlife where progression is stopped. For many, that thought does not sit well, so they create a belief that justifies their lack of understanding and actions. Others simply decide not to believe in God. An atheistic belief gives them the freedom to do what they want without consequence, but it also means that such freedom ends at death, in a nonexistent afterlife.

Both mind-sets can cause frustration. What I learned through fighting is that it's okay to lose a fight, and it's okay to not completely understand God. The important thing in fighting is that you learn from your mistakes and move on in an attempt to become the best fighter you can possibly be. That same logic applies as you attempt to find God. If you don't understand God perfectly, that's okay; just move on, learn from your mistakes, and experiment with different concepts and ideas concerning God until you have created a relationship with God that fills you with confidence and excitement. Because when you connect with the Creator of all things, it *will* fill you with confidence and excitement.

If the concept of God's existence collides with your scientific understanding of the universe, this does not destroy God's existence; it only means you must continue to use trial and error in discovering the truth concerning what seem like discrepancies. Trying to prove there is a God is impossible, so rather than give up on God because you can't prove He exists, continue to seek God through trial and error and by constantly asking questions. Then, allow yourself to gain a relationship with Him through your failures and misunderstandings. Be comfortable with the fact that you do not fully understand Him; no one does. The goal is to understand these questions better through trial and error. Please keep the questions we've talked about in mind as you read this book and go through life.

Once again, you need to understand that you cannot prove that God exists. You may find evidence, but evidence and proof are two different things. Once you are comfortable with your lack of proof, you can focus on finding evidence. Godly evidence comes through asking, searching, failing, and trying to find it over and over again. You must repeat this cycle until you have collected enough evidence to convince yourself you have found the truth behind these questions. I'm not out to prove anything. I simply want to show you how the principles of fighting have helped me understand how to find God.

I'm not saying this book can prove there is a God, but I promise you that reading this book will change the way you understand God and life.

Chapter 2

What Is the Best Martial Art?

THROUGHOUT THIS BOOK YOU'LL SEE how fighting and finding God are similar. As you read about fighting, ask yourself how it relates to God, and as you read about God, ask yourself how that relates to fighting. Once your mind opens to the concept, you will start to see common ground in many different areas. If you don't see the correlation immediately, keep reading, as I will point out the similarities throughout the book. Now, think about how you can discover God as I explain how I discovered the best way to fight.

My whole life, I wanted to know which martial art or sport best prepared someone for a real fight. Who doesn't want to know how to fight? It's one of the coolest hobbies ever. Growing up in an era without the internet, there were questions I assumed I would never know the answers to, like what the best martial art was.

As a five- to twelve-year-old boy, I was consumed with finding the answer to this question. But as a middle-class kid from Taylorsville, Utah, growing up in the 1980s and 1990s, I didn't have a lot of exposure to different styles of fighting. What little education I did have came from Saturday morning cartoons, Ninja Turtles, and X-Men. It also came from movies and video games—mostly *Street Fighter II* (and let's not forget fighting with my older brothers and play-fighting with friends).

In my youngest years, I thought karate might be the best martial art because of what I'd seen on television, in the movies, and in video games. But even if I had made up my mind and said, "Yes, karate is the best martial art," I would have had to find the best style of karate and the best local karate dojo.

There was no way my parents could afford to enroll me in any type of martial art classes, so I looked to my good friend the TV and wondered what other kinds of fighting there were—and I discovered pro wrestling! Professional wrestling was the best fight style ever because you could punch, kick, slam, use chairs as weapons, and jump off the ropes. Professional wrestling was great; it had to be the best fight style ever. Now I can't decide which was worse: finding out Santa was not real or that pro wrestling was fake. What kind of world do we live in where lying to kids seems to be the norm?

Back to the drawing board. I realized I could never trust my "good friend" again. Where could I turn in my quest to find the best martial art? It was around this time that my brothers joined their junior-high wrestling team. They would often sit in front of the television and drill the moves they learned at wrestling practice and talk about how awesome wrestling was. It made me wonder, *Is wrestling the best fight style ever?* I wanted it to be because I knew my brothers could teach me some sweet moves and I could also join a wrestling team in a few years. If it was the best martial art, I had access to it.

But as a young kid, I needed proof before I could believe it, so I tested wrestling techniques against the karate moves I'd learned watching television. I would punch and kick my brothers to see if their wrestling moves would work against the great art of karate. Without fail—because they were bigger than me and I didn't really know karate—they would grab me, pin me to the ground, and render me helpless. That convinced me wrestling was the best way to fight.

The problem was that wrestling was so boring to watch—no jump kicks and no flying off the ropes to slam your opponent. And the competitors wore goofy-looking singlets and rolled around on the ground. It was flat-out boring. But it was all I had, so I embraced it and learned all I could. And I eventually fell in love with it.

Yet, throughout junior high and high school, the internal debate went on and on. And I was not the only one who wanted to know what the best martial art was. There were countless times I had this debate with my friends. The kids who took karate class always thought the sport their parents were paying a hundred dollars a month for was the best. However, I quickly noticed that every fight I saw at school went to the ground. How could karate be the best way to fight when all the fights I saw in real life ended up on the ground? With wrestling, we learned how to maneuver on the ground in a combat situation, and it made sense to me that wrestling was an effective martial art.

When I was about fourteen, I started to gain ground on the subject when my friends and I learned about a fight league called the UFC—Ultimate Fighting Championship. This was a new kind of fighting. In its early days, the UFC only had three rules: no biting, no eye gouging, no groin strikes. When it came to *real* fighting, I had my answer. Whoever won the UFC was obviously using the best martial art!

When my friends and I had sleepovers at each other's houses, we would go to Blockbuster to rent movies. When we found out we could rent UFC videos, we watched them all night long. The problem was that we soon discovered there was no rhyme or reason to why some fighters won and others lost. I always cheered for the fighters who had a wrestling background because I had spent my teenage years on a wrestling team. I loved wrestling and wanted the art I'd spent so much time and energy learning to be the best.

Searching for one martial art was where I went wrong. My goal had always been to know which martial art was the best, *period*. I assumed only one art could be the best and that all I had to do was find it. Once I started fighting, it didn't take me long to realize I needed to have a goal in order to determine which fight style was best. My goals would dictate which art was best for me. If your goal is to be the best at punching, you should pursue boxing. If your goal is to be the best at all the stand-up techniques, such as punching, kicking, clinching, knees, and elbows, then Muay Thai is the art of choice. If your goal is to be the best at taking people down or avoiding takedowns, it's wrestling. And if your goal is to be the best at submission grappling, then look to jiu-jitsu. It's easy to see each art has a specialty and that no one art trumps the others; there are too many variables in a fight.

If you want to be a good fighter, you must learn all the arts.

The interesting thing is that each art has good and bad aspects in regard to MMA fighting. Let's take a look at wrestling. A wrestler's goal is to take their opponent down and pin that opponent's back to the ground. A bad habit wrestlers acquire is that when they take their opponent to the ground, they often stay between their opponent's legs. In the fight world, when you are on top, wrapped between your opponent's legs, you are in their guard. In a wrestling match, it's a good thing to take someone down and land on top in their guard. The guard position in a wrestling match can get you back points or maybe a pin. But in a fight, the guard position for the guy on top is not all that great because you risk getting put in triangle chokes, arm bars, and other submissions. This is one example of a habit wrestlers need to correct if they decide to fight MMA. When a wrestler gets a takedown in a fight, he must create a new habit of landing outside the opponent's legs or outside their guard. Getting a takedown and landing in guard is good for wrestling but bad for fighting. A good MMA fighter will take the best of all the arts, perfect the most useful fundamentals, and discard the habits that are only useful in that particular art.

There are reasons these martial arts hold on to useless moves, of which there are many within each art. First, many martial arts derive from combat sports with rules that were put in place to protect the athletes. Though the intention was good, anytime a rule is added to a combat sport, it takes away from what is considered real fighting. With rules, people develop habits that may enhance the combat sport yet take away from the true art of fighting.

Don't get me wrong. MMA *does* have rules; in addition to no groin strikes, eye gouging, or biting, there is no kicking or kneeing a grounded opponent in the head. There are no elbows that start straight up in the air and strike straight down. There is no grabbing the fence or stomping your opponent while the opponent is on the ground. There is no striking the back of the head or the spine. There are uniform standards fighters must abide by. Fighters also have to wear gloves issued by the promotion and fight shorts with no pockets. That doesn't cover all the MMA rules but most of the major ones. I'm not advocating for the elimination of rules for MMA. The rules have made MMA what it is today, but it's my belief that MMA is closer to true fighting than any other martial art.

Another reason martial arts have useless moves is that a lot of them are for show. That's fine. There is nothing wrong with fancy moves that show off athleticism, if that is your goal. Where many people go wrong is that they believe fancy, high-flying flips and kicks constitute real fighting.

Once again, we are faced with the concept of goals. The only true way to find the best martial art for you is to understand your goals when it comes to fighting. If your goal is to be a great all-around fighter, MMA obviously is the best choice.

You could pursue street fighting, which is the most real fighting ever, but then you could be faced with jail time, lawsuits, and serious injury or death, all of which take away from your ability to train and improve as a fighter. Meanwhile, in MMA, doctors are present, blood is tested to avoid the transmission of disease, and there are just enough rules to keep fighters safe so they can compete often. And let's not forget you can get paid. When it comes to fighting, MMA is as close as you can legally get.

Some martial arts have developed very strange techniques. These are an example of how we can be influenced by our environment. People will believe crazy things about fighting because of something they saw on YouTube or were taught in a fight class. People often blindly believe things without personally testing the techniques.

One of my favorite things about fighting is learning something new. I'll grab someone at the gym and say, "Hey, I just learned a new move.

Let's fight. I want to see if I can get it to work." If I can get the move to work consistently when sparring, odds are it will work in a fight.

Another thing I do is watch other good fighters. If I see good fighters effectively use a particular move in a real fight, I gain confidence in that move.

A good fighter must commit to personal study, testing different techniques, and learning from others. A good fighter stays humble and teachable, yet is not ignorant of foolish traditions. If you keep your fighting goals in mind as you learn and grow as a fighter, you'll avoid the downfall of wasting time drilling useless techniques.

I continuously try to ask myself, "Will this movement actually help me win a fight?"

If the answer is yes, I keep practicing it. If I'm not sure, I get to the bottom of it through trial and error. If I find it's not a beneficial technique, I move on to something I know will help me as a fighter. Training hard is great, but training smart is better; it's important not to fall into the trap of training hard on useless techniques. Training smart is key, and understanding your goals is the only way you can train smart. You become a great fighter by training hard *and* smart, with a constant focus on your fight goals.

Chapter 3
Finding God

Can we use the same principles in finding the best fight style in our quest to find God? I have been fascinated not only with discovering the best way to fight but with the best way to find God. What could be more important than the ability to protect the ones you love and connect with God? As a matter of fact, if you have read the Bible, you'll know that is the premise of the whole book. Prophets have connected with God, and armies have been built up to protect the people who follow the prophets and God.

Under this logic you can see how finding God and self-defense work together. One of the biggest tragedies we see in the Bible is when people find God and then lose the right to serve and worship Him. One example is in the Old Testament in 2 Kings 24–25 when the house of Israel was overtaken by Babylon. Another couple of examples are the stories of Daniel in the lion's den and of Meshach, Shadrach, and Abednego, as found in Daniel chapters 3 and 6. If you don't know the stories, read them.

As you read the Bible, you will find plenty of stories about people who find God and then struggle to preserve their right to worship Him. As I read my scriptures, I see the need to discover God and preserve my right to worship Him. The connection between the art of fighting and the act of finding God is fascinating. What could be more important than finding God and then being able to freely worship Him as you see fit? There are times when we must fight to preserve that important freedom.

If you want to use the principles found in finding the best fight style and apply them to finding God and preserving the right to worship Him, there are seven key factors that must be in place:

1. Goals

My goals are based on the questions I asked in chapter 1:

Is there a God?

Who is God?

Where did I come from?

Where am I going?

Can I prove there is a God?

What does God expect of me?

How will God communicate with me?

2. Access to Information

Only when you have access to information can light be shed on these questions. It is information that opens our minds to all the possibilities out there. The information we receive may not always be true, but it's a starting point that gets the ball rolling so you can track down the right information.

In the past, the acquisition of information—especially regarding God—was hard to come by. In many ancient civilizations, cities, and countries, freedom of religion was a foreign idea. Even if you lived in a place that allowed religious freedom, you were still faced with limited information. Many people could not read, and they were often left to believe whatever they were told. If they could read, they were often left with a small library to choose from. So access to religious knowledge was, for the most part, very restricted for the average person, at least until the American Revolution.

Let's think about American history for a moment. The Pilgrims came to the New World in pursuit of religious freedom, having first escaped the Church of England by fleeing to Holland in 1609. While in Holland they found religious freedom yet struggled to find a prosperous lifestyle. They also didn't like the influence the new culture was having on their children. Lastly, and maybe most importantly, war loomed between Holland and Spain, and the Pilgrims did not want to be involved.

Under the leadership of William Bradford, they left for the New World on the *Mayflower* and on the *Speedwell* in 1620. After the *Speedwell* experienced leaks on two occasions, both ships headed back to England, where they crammed the passengers from the *Speedwell* onto the *Mayflower* and completed their journey on November 11, 1620. They landed in Cape Cod, and then a few weeks later went to Plymouth, where they put down their roots. It was an absolute miracle the natives did not run them out of town immediately.

If we fast-forward to the Revolutionary War, on April 19, 1775, we find the American colonists facing the British forces. A year later, Congress approves the Declaration of Independence on July 4, 1776. The war ends, and America finally gains its independence on September 3, 1783. Once again—an absolute miracle.

The American Revolution set the perfect backdrop for the religious revival of the eighteen hundreds with the American people now having access to religious information and the freedom to worship in any way they chose. The printing press became a common piece of technology, and the Bible was produced at an unprecedented rate. Living in America signified many different opportunities for those interested in finding God.

Among the Americans enjoying these new opportunities was the founder and first prophet of The Church of Jesus Christ of Latter-day Saints, Joseph Smith. Whether or not you believe Joseph Smith's story, it illustrates how we can all discover God when we have access to information.

In the early eighteen hundreds surrounding the Vermont and New York area where Joseph Smith grew up, a great deal of religious revival was going on. Caught up in this religious awakening, fourteen-year-old Joseph found himself searching for answers, but there were so many churches offering different points of view on the various doctrines found in the scriptures that he became stuck. In his confusion, he looked to the Bible and discovered James 1:5: "If any of you lack wisdom, let him ask of God, that giveth to all men liberally, and upbraideth not; and it shall be given him." Joseph decided to do exactly as the scripture directed—ask of God. And so he went to a nearby grove of trees to ask which religious sect was true—assuming one had to be. He honestly thought there must be one correct religion patterned after the church Christ established while on the earth.

Joseph Smith–History 1:15–17 gives us the account of how Joseph went alone into the grove, knelt down, and began to pray aloud, attempting to ask which of the religions of his day was true. Immediately he was "seized upon by some unseen power" that bound his tongue, and "thick darkness" gathered around him. It seemed for a time he was doomed to destruction. Joseph was ready to sink into despair and "abandon himself to destruction" but began "exerting all his power to call upon God" to deliver him from this enemy (verse 16). At this moment, Joseph saw a glorious light and describes what he saw:

> I saw a pillar of light exactly over my head, above the brightness of the sun, which descended gradually until it fell upon me. It no sooner appeared than I found myself delivered from the enemy which held me bound. When the light rested upon me I saw two Personages, whose brightness and glory defy all description, standing above me in the air. One of them spake unto me, calling me by name and said, pointing to the other— This is my beloved son. Hear him! (verses 16–17)

The Lord told Joseph he must join none of the churches and that Joseph would be the one to establish Jesus Christ's true church in the latter days, or modern times.

The American Revolution is one of my all-time favorite periods of history. America gained its independence against all odds, and the resulting republic became a place that not only promoted freedom and democracy but catapulted the early colonists to economic success. As people settled and built various businesses, development increased at a rapid rate. Printing presses got to work. There was a boom in education and increased access to information. The miracles taking place in American history allowed Joseph Smith the opportunity and the right to read James 1:5 as well as the freedom to pray and ask God which church was true.

We have the same opportunity today. We have access to information and the freedom to investigate. In fact, we face a unique problem—we have more information than ever before. Our investigation process is more about eliminating information than finding ways to access it. So, with all we have at our fingertips, how do we start investigating God in an efficient manner? As you read, we will discuss ways to investigate God without wasting precious time on useless information.

3. An Open Mind

People often have a preconceived notion of what God is. They already have an identity for God. A preconceived identity of God can come from many different sources—parents, family, friends, church, school, the media—or a combination of these things. The God you have created in your mind through the world's influence may not be the God who actually exists.

Let's use Joseph Smith's experience as an example. Again, you may not believe his story, but it illustrates a good point. Joseph had a preconceived notion. He thought God already had a true church on the earth. Through his experience in the grove, he realized he had to open his mind to a new concept. Joseph learned that God's true identity had been lost to man throughout history. It would be his responsibility to introduce the world to the same God Abraham, Isaac, and Jacob worshiped. Restoring God's truth to the earth was a unique concept to Joseph, but his being able to have an open mind to these spiritual experiences was possible because of his freedom to learn, pray, and experiment on God's word.

In my various conversations with people about God, I've learned that many already have an identity for God. It can be very difficult for someone to turn from the idea they already have and accept a new idea of God. I had to redefine God when I read the Old Testament. Anyone who has read the Old Testament can probably relate. Being raised Mormon my whole life, I began to paint a picture in my mind of who and what God was. I'd become comfortable with the God I'd created in my mind, and it shook my whole world when I finally read the Old Testament as an adult and had to redefine who God was. Through prayer and study, I realized many of the things I'd always believed about God were wrong and that I could never be satisfied with my understanding of God.

You will never fully understand God in this life. If you think you fully understand Him, you are wrong. You don't. If you do fully and completely understand God, it means you're a god, because only a god can comprehend all the things the Lord God can comprehend (see Mosiah 4:9). The best thing we can do is to continually try to better understand God throughout our lives and not get stuck in the rut of assuming we know who He is.

I have seen many people back themselves into a corner and think that if their belief in God is not exact and perfect, they will be sentenced to hell because they do not understand Him correctly. There are billions of people on the earth, and everyone understands and believes in God differently. Your understanding of God is a lot like your fingerprint; it is unique to you. No one sees or understands God the way you do. Because no one fully understands God, does that lack of understanding mean we are all going to hell? We all believe differently; we can't all be right. Even people from the same religion view and understand God in different ways. How can we know our eternal destination when everyone understands God so differently?

I believe God is a God of love; He acts in love and is motivated by love. God is more concerned with our faith in Him than our belief and knowledge of Him. I believe God is concerned with our faith in Him because none of us can comprehend Him in this life. Yet, it pleases God when we look to Him, worship Him, and serve others in an attempt to serve Him. The essence of faith is believing in God even though you recognize you do not wholly understand Him, then developing a belief in God that promotes a loving lifestyle.

Our faith and God's love combined allow us to sin and have misunderstandings. Because God loves us, a perfect knowledge and a perfect life are not required. Our final judgment won't be based on perfection. Our final judgment will be based on the perfect love and understanding of an all-knowing and loving God. If God is motivated by love, certainly He's provided a way for us to return to Him even though we do not correctly understand Him. If I'm right, there is wiggle room and an opportunity to experiment with beliefs without fear of being condemned to hell for misunderstanding. The important thing is that we are loving, caring people who exercise faith and who serve others and God.

4. Humility

People often live life to its fullest, thinking only of themselves and of what they want from it. Once they have established a lifestyle that suits them, they look for a god who is okay with it. Throughout history, people have created some very unusual gods. Entire cultures have fallen in love with lustful practices and created gods who are okay with those practices. Creating a self-pleasing god, a comfortable god, happens when individuals try to feel good about their particular lifestyle. Creating a god who is okay with the way you live your life is the path of least resistance.

Another thing I have seen people do is create a god who does not exist at all, aka atheism. Never in human history has atheism been so widespread. It makes sense that this is such a popular philosophy these days—if you can convince yourself there is no God, you need never feel guilt. You can live your life however you want.

Many say atheism is growing because of science and knowledge. Scientific discovery does not disprove God; it only shows the God you thought you knew and the God who actually exists may be different. I have had many conversations with people about how the latest in science and physics proves there is no God, and I always walk away thinking, *Wow, God is more powerful than I thought*. New scientific knowledge does not void God's existence; it only shows what little we know about Him.

It's convenient: if you don't want a God, you just put Him in a box. Then, with the god you have created and stuffed in a box, you can say, "Look, science and God are different." But with that concept you can also say, "Yep, I knew it; God is greater than we thought." Yes, you can say that if you want a God.

If you don't want a God, you can do the opposite. Every time we learn and discover something, you can say, "Yep, I knew it. This new discovery proves God can't exist." If you don't want a God, you will do whatever necessary to prove to yourself that there is no God. With no God comes no guilt, and no guilt means you can live however you want. But the most convenient lifestyle is not the goal. The goal is to find God and then figure out what God expects of you.

Humility means we are willing to accept God regardless of previous beliefs. Our goal is to find the true God and then figure out how God communicates with us. Once we have found God and have learned how to communicate with Him, we must be humble enough to do what He expects of us to grow closer to the true God we have discovered. It takes humility and an open mind to find God. I promise there is something you and I believe about God that is wrong. I can say this because I often find myself learning new things about our Creator.

If my belief never evolved with life experiences, I would still believe in a God who lives on a cloud surrounded by angels playing harps.

It may seem arrogant for me to say "There is something you believe about God that is wrong." I'm not saying I know more about God than you do. If you knew more about God than anyone, you still would not fully understand God; there would still be more for you to learn and more corrections you would need to make to your current understanding.

Let's get real. Do you really think when you die you will find yourself in your new realm of existence and think, *Yeah, this is exactly what I thought it would be like?* And when you meet your Creator, do you think there will be no surprising knowledge obtained? Do you think after meeting the Great Organizer of all we know you will think, *Yep, that's exactly what I thought God would be like?* The notion that we might fully know God in this life is crazy.

Once you can admit you don't understand God, you are in a position to find Him.

Can you admit you don't fully understand God? Can you admit there is something you currently believe about God that may be wrong? Accepting correction is difficult. When an incorrect belief is discovered, are you humble enough to change your belief system, even if it means changing your lifestyle? If having an open mind means being willing to accept new ideas, being humble would mean being willing to act on the new concepts you learn to be true.

5. Learning from Others

Learning from others is usually the most convenient and easy way to learn. You can let someone else do the homework and the experimenting. Let others make the mistakes so you don't have to. Learn from those who have gone before and who can teach you valuable lessons. With all the information we have concerning God, the biggest challenge is not finding information; it's filtering information and figuring out which information is true.

People are often quick to offer their opinions about who God is and what He's like. All you have to do is ask. Sure, there are some who may shy away from such conversation, but I have found most everyone has an opinion. Often when people shy away it's because they think I'm going to push my views on them. But when they see I'm truly interested in their point of view, they start to open up.

Here are a few questions I ask myself as I'm filtering the information I learn from others:

Do I trust this person?

Why do they believe these things?

What motivates their belief? Is it love, money, lifestyle, or some crazy reason?

Sometimes people just want to prove they are right. Others like to hear themselves talk, and if you sit and listen, they will say just about anything to hear what they have to say. It's not hard to tell whether someone's motives are selfish or altruistic. If their motives are selfish, their opinions can easily be corrupted through selfish reasoning. If someone is motivated by love, they live a God-centered life. You could even have two people both motivated by love, and still have two totally different views on God. How then would you be able to find truth?

Many people in my life have brought me closer to God. The people who have really helped me gain a stronger understanding of God are people who have giving and caring attributes. The people that have helped me find God are giving of their time and money; they are willing to sacrifice their wants to serve and help others.

Finding God is different for each of us, and we are all at different levels of understanding. It's not like going to your dad's favorite restaurant, and when the waitress asks, "Do you need time to look at the menu?" your dad jumps in and says, "Nope, we will take two number fives." Whatever—eat what your dad thinks is the best. It's no big deal. He is probably paying for it anyway.

Finding God is different. We can't let people tell us what to believe. But if you see godly attributes in a person, try to figure out what they know and believe and how they came to their conclusions. Once you obtain good information from those who care about you, it's up to you to figure out whether or not what you've learned is true.

When learning from others, we need to obtain the information, keep an open mind, stay humble, and experiment on the words of those we trust. And hopefully through the experiences and knowledge of others, we can accelerate our understanding of God.

6. Testing the Information Personally

All we need to do is learn everything anyone has ever learned about God and then put everyone's opinions to the test, right? The fact is, there is not enough time to test everyone's opinions. Where does this leave us? How do we figure out which information is worthy of our time? Let's recall the key points we talked about earlier.

First, our foremost goal is to know these things:

Is there a God?

Who is God?

Where did I come from?

Where am I going?

Can I prove there is a God?

What does God expect of me?

How will God communicate with me?

Second, we need access to information. We need the ability to learn from many different sources.

Third, we need to keep an open mind. We can't assume we already know or assume something is automatically right or wrong.

Fourth, we need to understand the importance of humility. We need to be willing to admit we are wrong and, if necessary, change our current lifestyle in order to grow closer to God.

Fifth, we should always be learning from others, especially from those who care about us and those we trust so we don't have to spend so much time learning the hard way.

So, what information is worthy of my time? What information should I test? I don't know of a belief system that says you can't talk to God. Every person I have ever talked to who believes in God agrees regular communication with Him is important. An atheist may say you can't talk to God because God doesn't exist. But that is like me saying you can't talk to a rock because the rock is not listening. Even if the rock is not listening, you can still talk to the rock. Even if an atheist says you can't talk to God because God does not exist, you still have the freedom to talk to God. Remember the question "What is worthy of my time in trying to discover God?" Talking to God on a personal level is most definitely something you should do. Test this information, and talk to God.

If there is a God, and God is all powerful (I think God would be all powerful because He would be the one responsible for creating the heavens and the earth), why not ask God if He exists? That's right, just ask. Try it right now. Put the book down and ask out loud if God is there. Then listen! Be quiet and *listen*. Open your mind to all the possibilities. Think about the heavens and the earth and all things from the beginning of time. Try to imagine what it might have been like in the beginning of time before the big bang—in a time where matter was without form or purpose.

Was there a Great Organizer, one who held power over all the elements and who created the heavens and the earth? Did God create the universe and all the galaxies, even our galaxy? Did God create our solar system? Did God create our sun, making it the perfect size, and place the earth at the perfect distance from the sun? Did God tilt the earth with the perfect axis and give it just the right rotation? Did God give us a moon that is just the right size, and rotates at just the right speed and at the right distance from the earth? Was it God who created an earth with all the right conditions to support life? Is God the one responsible for perfect DNA sequencing? Did God put life in motion and guide it to what we see and know today?

As you think about these things, open your mind and allow the Almighty Creator to have an influence over your thoughts; see what it is God wants you to know. If God is the one responsible for countless creations, He must have powers and abilities beyond our comprehension. Let the all-powerful Creator have a place in your mind. Allow God to answer your questions. Remember that God is beyond our realm of existence and comprehension. He has the ability to communicate with you in many different ways. Let God be God and communicate with you the way He sees fit.

We live in a physical world where we can see, hear, smell, touch, and taste. If God created the world, He must have almighty power over all things physical. Surely He could use our five senses to convince us of His existence by using the world around us to do so. Or maybe our existence is the only evidence we need to know there is a Great Creator. So the evidence is the fact that we are alive today, but what we want is proof.

If God created all things, He is definitely living on a higher plane of existence than we are—not only with power over our physical universe but with power over a higher level of existence beyond what we can comprehend. What would that higher level of existence be like? Obviously, without the physical ability to sense it, we cannot tap into God's higher plane of comprehension.

Or can we? That is the test. Can we talk to God in these special moments of solitude? As we reach out to our Creator, can we be brought to a higher level of understanding, a level of knowledge beyond words or description? Could that elevated comprehension be the proof we are looking for? Could higher understanding be the proof that is sufficient because you felt the godly presence in your being, yet because it was not physical, it was lost to the rest of the world? It's not proof, because we can't prove it to anyone. Yet you know *it* because you felt *it*, and the frustrating thing is that words can't describe *it*. You are the only one who can understand *it*. What a gift this would be—soul-piercing proof that God exists—proof that is yours and yours only. It would be an understanding found only by those who diligently seek to find God. It would be a truth preserved for those willing to accept His presence in whatever way God chooses to reveal Himself. If you discover God and gain an understanding of His reality, you then may be led to ask exactly who and what He is and what He expects of you.

What is your relationship to God? Some say He is our father. There are many definitions of the word *father*. One that sticks out to me is "to assume or admit responsibility for something." Another is "one who creates or is the founder of something." If God is the one responsible for us, created all we know, and is the founder of our physical existence, He would be, by the above definition, my father and your father. If He is our Father, is there an element of love? Is God motivated by love? Ask Him if His creative purpose is motivated by love. Does our Father have a plan for us motivated by His love for us? As my goals have dictated, I don't just want to know if there is a God; I want to know who God is and what He expects of me.

If the experiment worked and you have discovered that there is a God, that He is your Father, and that He loves you, you have now found a formula for communicating with God. With this formula you can now find answers to many questions. One of the most important things you can learn is what God expects of you and how He wants you to live your life. If you know what it feels like to draw near to God, you can pay close attention to the way different activities make you feel. Do these activities draw you closer to God or pull you away from Him?

If you can discover God by opening your mind and soul to Him, you can have spirit-to-spirit moments with your Creator. Earlier we called it a higher plane of comprehension. Call it whatever you want—God has the highest of all power, authority, and intelligence. He can elevate your ability to learn beyond your natural, physical faculties. God can elevate and teach you beyond what the physical world can, beyond what your physical mind can comprehend. We can call these spiritual moments, moments where your spirit and God's spirit unite to enlighten your mind and inspire your actions.

There is no doubt our physical world exists. We can all prove that fact. But in these moments of drawing near to God and getting a glimpse of His magnificence, we begin to see the evidence of a spiritual plane. It is evidence that with time can be known as a personal truth. We live in a physical world and have been talking about ways to elevate our minds to a spiritual plane.

I mentioned testing information personally. When you test information personally, your life becomes an everyday experiment. What in your life creates spiritual moments? What in your life limits your ability to grow? Do you have friends who lift you up and make you feel good about yourself? Or do you have friends who are fun yet leave you feeling empty and disappointed in yourself? How do you feel when you lift others? How do you feel when you cut others down?

Pay attention to how you feel as you talk to different people, read different books, and participate in different types of entertainment. Things that elevate you will connect you to your spirit and draw you closer to God. Things that drag you down will pull you away from Him. The hard part is being disciplined enough to put yourself in situations and take notes on how different things and activities make you feel. The good thing is you probably already have an idea from past experience what elevates you and brings you true, lasting happiness and what makes you feel empty, dirty, and unhappy.

7. Not Wasting Time on Useless Traditions

We haven't talked about religious traditions. Religion is not my goal; my goal is God. Some may say because I asked you to pray we're talking about a religious tradition. Well, I didn't ask you to pray. I asked you to talk to God. What's the difference? The difference is the tradition we often find in prayer. If you were taught as a child the structure of prayer and you often don't pray because of the necessity to be formal, then the formality of that type of prayer has become counterproductive. I don't want you praying to God or even worshiping God. What I want is for you to have a conversation with Him.

There are activities that bring you closer to God and activities that don't. What you want to do is find things that bring you closer to Him. If you can find God on your own, when it comes time to unite yourself with a group of people who also claim to know God, you will be able to recognize whether their motives and activities are God-centered or not.

Many have asked me, "Why would I need a group of people in order to grow closer to God? If I can find God on my own, why not continue to worship on my own?"

The answer is found in the word *teamwork*. Fight teams are a good example of why we are better off surrounding ourselves with others working toward the same goals. Your fight team helps push you to the next level. They get you out of bed in the morning for morning practice and motivate you to work harder than you would by yourself. They also give you an opportunity to practice in live situations with sparring rounds and drilling moves. You learn from your teammates, and your teammates learn from you.

The other principle I like that relates is that inevitably it does come down to just you. In a fight it's only you in the cage—no team. It is just you and your opponent; it's all up to you at that point. But your fight team helped you become the athlete you are in those moments of battle.

Finding God is similar. Good, honest people who have also found a connection with God will help you build a stronger relationship with Him. However, like in a fight, it eventually comes down to the personal relationship you build with God in those private moments as you wrestle with Him in prayer.

Keeping your focus on God is a great way to avoid wasting time on things that don't matter. And time is precious! Why? If you live to be seventy-eight (the average US life expectancy), you will have lived

4,056 weeks (multiply seventy-eight by fifty-two). You will have lived 936 months. You will have lived 28,470 days. Now let's look at the hours. You will have seen 683,280 hours. We have 683,280 hours to figure out whether or not God lives and, if He does, what He expects of us.

But we don't really have 683,280 hours to find God. We sleep, work, eat, clean, and fix things. There is health and hygiene to take care of, and there are the hobbies we enjoy. We are lucky if we get an hour a day to ourselves, which gives us 28,470 hours to find and connect with God. Most of us only have an hour a week, which would only give us 4,056 hours to find and connect with God. With such limited time to discover and align ourselves with our Creator, it's important we make God a high priority and not waste time on useless traditions. Discovering God is a lifelong process, but we don't know how long our life is. We cannot afford to waste it; we need to discover God now. When you get together with others who claim to know God, what are you doing with them? Hopefully the teammates you choose to spend time with in serving God are using their time wisely. It would be a shame if you had to look back on your life and realize you wasted much of your precious time in false and foolish traditions.

What are false and foolish traditions? That's what you need to figure out. Many religious groups have traditions that I don't see how they could bring a person closer to God. On the flip side, many non-religious groups have traditions I do think would bring a person closer to God. Regardless of the group or the group's affiliation, focus on the goal: finding God. The goal of this book is to help you create a God-centered life so your thoughts and opinions align with His. My opinions may not be aligned perfectly with God, but let me share what I have found through my spiritual experiments. Trying to align our will with God's will can be hard. What we want and what God expects of us can be very different. When we pursue selfish goals, we feel a disconnect from God. Through my spiritual experiments, I have found that I experience spiritual enlightenment when I'm serving and helping others.

I have never regretted serving others, even when it costs me time and money. When it comes to selfish things, trust me, I have plenty of regrets. What I have found through spiritual experimentation is that service is key in connecting with God. When it comes to associating with people who claim to know God, I ask, "Do these people strive to help others?"

I would never consider service a false or foolish tradition. I can honestly say I'm not always excited to serve, but I can also say that once I'm finished serving, I'm always glad I did. It reminds me of working out. I'm not always excited to work out, but when I do, I always feel better about myself.

If you want to use fight principles to discover God, you need goals, access to information, an open mind, a good dose of humility, a willingness to learn from others, a desire to test information personally, and the determination to avoid wasting time on useless traditions. Through analyzing these principles, we see how spiritual experiments can help us discover which activities align our actions with God's will. Now that you have an understanding of God and His will, you can look for friends and groups of people who will help you pursue God-centered goals regardless of what those people call themselves, whether it be a religion or some other type of group. My goal is to find others who will help me grow closer to God using useful God-centered traditions.

Chapter 4
Fundamentals

My two greatest passions in life are combat sports and my faith. As different as these two passions seem to be, I am constantly finding principles in fighting that parallel the principles of the gospel of Jesus Christ. Let's begin with the fundamentals of fighting. Hand-to-hand combat has four major elements.

Striking

Typically, striking is fighting while you and your opponent are on your feet and is often referred to as Muay Thai, which includes punching, kicking, clinch, knees, and elbows.

Wrestling

I like to define wrestling as the art of taking your opponent down and not allowing that opponent to take you down.

Submission Grappling

Submission grappling is putting your opponent in a position where they are faced with the decision either to give up and tap out or risk serious injury or death.

Ground and Pound

I call ground and pound the lost art. It involves punching, kicking, kneeing, and elbowing your opponent while you and your opponent are on the ground or just your opponent is on the ground and you stand above and strike down.

All four of the above fighting arts have fundamental principles and techniques that must be ingrained in a fighter's mind and perfected for him or her to become a good fighter.

Also all four arts have complex components that can be effective and fun to study, practice, and use. But before you jump into the complexity of these arts, you must first perfect the fundamentals.

To become a great fighter, you must first study, then practice the fundamentals of the four arts, then perfect the techniques within each of them. And you can't just study one art and expect to be a good fighter; you must study and practice all the arts. If you focus all your attention on one style of fighting, you may become really good at that style of fighting, but you will lack experience in the other areas of fighting which can put you at a big disadvantage.

Now, let's find the parallel principles in the gospel. I'm going to compare the fighting arts to the gospel of Jesus Christ as taught by The Church of Jesus Christ of Latter-day Saints (LDS). I use the LDS Church for two reasons. First, as mentioned, the LDS Church is the one I grew up in and the one I am the most familiar with. Second, the programs within the LDS Church are efficient and get results.

In The Church of Jesus Christ of Latter-day Saints, we have what is called the "fourfold mission of the Church":

Perfect the Saints

Perfecting the Saints means being active in your church assignments. By being active in church assignments, we are given opportunities to serve and teach other members within the Church.

Proclaim the Gospel

Proclaiming the gospel is sharing the message of Jesus Christ with those who don't understand what Christ has done for them. We invite everyone to come unto Christ. For those who are willing to learn, we teach them of Christ's restored gospel.

Redeem the Dead

Members of the LDS Church believe that every single soul who has ever lived upon the earth is a child of God and, as such, should have the opportunity to receive the ordinances we believe enable us to experience ultimate joy and peace. In doing genealogy, we seek out the names of those who came before us. We then take those names to the temple and do proxy work for these people that didn't have the chance to be baptized or take the name of Christ upon them while in this life. Ultimately, those who have passed on to the other side and whom the work is done for have the freedom to decide whether to accept that work or not (see Malachi 4:6).

Care for the Poor and Needy

The different organizations within the LDS Church are constantly arranging service projects members can participate in. There are also different charities we are given the opportunity to donate to within the Church. In addition, we are encouraged to seek out and help the poor and needy in our local area.

Now, similar to the fighting principles, these four missions have both complex and simple sides. Perfecting the fundamentals prepares us to move on to deeper knowledge and greater responsibilities as we serve God. To become a true disciple of Christ, much like a fighter follows a coach, we must follow His example in all things. Let's go more in depth about how Christ is the Great Exemplar of these four missions of the Church.

Perfect the Saints

In the New Testament, Christ goes into the synagogue and teaches the gospel (see Luke 4). Those He teaches are members of the house of Israel who know the gospel due to their lineage. These people from the tribe of Judah, or Jews, would have been able to trace their genealogy back to King David, Moses, Judah, Israel, Isaac, Abraham, Noah, and eventually back to Adam and Eve. These people knew the prophets and had the scriptures. They also would have been familiar with the prophecies of Isaiah that spoke of the coming Messiah. In short, Christ taught those who were already familiar with the gospel.

Proclaim the Gospel

Up to the time of Christ, the gospel was only taught among the house of Israel, or those with the birthright who were born into the Abrahamic Covenant. In John chapter 4, Jesus teaches a woman of Samaria, which was a significant departure from who He had been teaching. Who were the Samaritans, and who was this woman?

The land called Samaria lay north of Jerusalem and was occupied by Israelites until about 734 BC. By Israelites I am referring to those who were related to the Jews through Israel, those who would have been from one of the twelve tribes of Israel. The Assyrians invaded the north part of Israel in 734 BC and took those tribes into captivity. Ten of the tribes of Israel were lost at this point. But the southern part of Israel—the tribe of Judah, aka the Jews—was preserved by the Lord. Then, in 609 BC, Babylon took up arms against the struggling Assyrians, and power shifted from the Assyrians to the Babylonians. If you remember the story of Daniel and the lion's den, it took place at the time Babylon took over not just the northern Assyrian country but also the southern country occupied by Judah. Daniel, Meshach, Shadrach, and Abednego were some of the righteous Jews who were preserved.

When the Persian army fell upon Babylon in 539 BC, power shifted once again. At this point, the Lord had compassion upon the Jews and inspired Cyrus, king of the Persians, to allow the Jews to return to Jerusalem, as prophesied by Isaiah (see Isaiah 44:28). This set the stage for the relationship between the Jews and the Samaritans. The

Jews had been through some trying times, yet they still kept most of their doctrines and bloodline intact due to righteous men like Daniel. But as for the territory north of Jerusalem, which was occupied by the Samaritans, it had once been Israel and was made up of the different tribes of Israel lost during the Assyrian takeover. The Samaritans not only had mixed blood but mixed traditions and religions. You can see why the Jews, being of pure blood and pure religion, considered the Samaritans beneath them.

However, this did not affect Christ's judgment at all. In a time when it was unacceptable for a Jewish man to teach a Samaritan woman, Christ was not influenced by the traditions of the Jews but by the love He had for all God's children. This is a great example of Christ proclaiming the gospel to a non-Jewish person. After the Crucifixion and Resurrection, our perfected, glorified Savior commissioned His apostles to "go . . . and teach all nations" (Matthew 28:19).

Redeem the Dead

As mentioned, redeeming the dead is done in the temples today. Our Savior loved the temple. In Luke 2:41–52 we read that when He was twelve, His parents traveled to Jerusalem for the Passover. When it was over, they had gone a day's journey toward home when they realized He was not with them. They returned to look for Him, and three days later found Him in the temple. When they found Him, His mother essentially asked, "Where have you been? What are you doing?" And Jesus basically answered, "Did you look for me at the temple? Of course I would be about my Father's business."

As an adult, Christ went to the temple and rebuked the money changers (see Matthew 21:12–16). He also went to the temple to teach by day and to the Mount of Olives to pray by night (see Luke 21:37).

Christ loved the temple, but where does redeeming the dead come into play? In John 5:25, Christ tells us the dead shall hear the voice of the Son of God. In 1 Corinthians 15, Paul explains that Christ was raised from the dead, then asks, "Why are they then baptized for the dead?" Peter also gives us an example of Christ doing work for the dead. 1 Peter 2:18–20 tells us that when Christ was put to death in the flesh, He went to preach to the spirits in prison. He also explains that the gospel was preached to those who were dead (see 4:6). Christ loves all mankind, living and dead.

Care for the Poor and Needy

The Gospels in the New Testament are chock-full of examples of how Christ cared for the poor and needy. Some of my favorites are found in Matthew 8–9; Mark 2, 5–8; Luke 5–7; and John 5–6, which are mentioned later in my book. If your goal is to truly understand how to find God, you'll need to read these scriptures to see how caring for the poor and needy is fundamental to your search.

Now let's see how fighting and the Gospel can be similar. To master the fundamentals of striking, you must be in shape and capable of explosive and dynamic movements over a long period of time. A fighter must work out every day to stay in tip-top shape, drilling fundamental moves and developing muscle memory. Muscle memory is what allows a fighter to keep performing with proper technique even when the fight is exhausting.

In perfecting the Saints, the goal is to help members serve, teach, and participate in activities. To serve others, you must pray for opportunities to serve and be willing to serve. To teach, you must study and acquire knowledge. To help others be active in church, you must be active yourself. The key to effectively perfecting the Saints lies in studying the scriptures, praying daily and going to church weekly.

Take a look at the remaining fighting arts and their fundamentals and how they align with the rest of the missions of the Church and their fundamentals.

> The key elements of *wrestling* are working out daily to develop endurance, strength, and muscle memory. The key elements of *proclaiming the gospel* are studying and praying daily and going to church weekly.

The key elements of *submission grappling* are working out daily to develop endurance, strength, and muscle memory. The key elements of *redeeming the dead* are studying and praying daily and going to church weekly.

The key elements of *ground and pound* are working out daily to develop endurance, strength, and muscle memory. The key elements of *caring for the poor and needy* are studying and praying daily and going to church weekly.

It's not hard to figure out. Consistent hard work over a long period of time is the key to success in all things. If you look at the key elements of fighting, you see a direct relationship between your work ethic and developing your talent.

It may not be as easy to see how studying the gospel, praying, and going to church assist in some of the Church's missions. How can these activities help you to perfect the Saints, share the gospel, redeem the dead, and care for the poor and needy?

Fighting is a very physical sport—the most physically demanding sport, period. It can be like long-distance running because some bouts last up to twenty-five minutes. Fighting is also a bit like strength training because often you need to lift an opponent who is as big and as strong as you are. And this battle of endurance and strength is being played out while you are being hit, kicked, and slammed to the ground.

Physical talents are developed through hard work and continual practice. Spiritual talents are developed by doing spiritual things. Being a disciple of Christ is a spiritual talent. Studying the scriptures, praying, and going to church are fundamental to developing spiritual talents. If you don't believe me, try it. Read your scriptures. If you read what I asked you to read, you will have had the chance to walk with Christ and envision what it may have been like to serve and help people the way He did.

When I read about how Jesus was able to help people with the touch of His hand, it makes me want to feel what Christ felt when He brought relief to those who suffered. The authority of Christ was powerful. It was often just a touch or a quick prayer that brought relief to the suffering or food to the hungry. I wish I could have been there and seen these miracles myself. I want to be a part of what Christ felt as He brought relief to the captive.

I can't perform miracles the way Christ did, but I have found that when I help others to the best of my ability, I feel peace. I've wondered during these times of service if the peace I felt was a portion of what Christ felt during His ministry. If so, then it makes all the sense in the world why so many people followed Him. I try to imagine being there to witness His miracles and feeling the peace of His spirit. Just reading the stories about it makes me want to follow Him. Can you see how reading your scriptures can motivate you to act and serve?

Communicating with God through prayer has a similar effect on me. Discussing the events in my life with God helps me clear my mind. Getting on my knees and saying my prayers has helped me prioritize my life. We all have many things going on in life—family, work, school, friends, and hobbies. At times when I find myself off track spending too much time on things of little importance, if I get on my knees and discuss these things with God, the many different activities I have going on start to fall into place as far as priority. Prayer has been the tool that gets my life back in order.

Think about the scriptures you just read (Matthew 8–9; Mark 2, 5–8; Luke 5–7; and John 5–6). Did reading of Christ instill a desire to serve others? Perhaps. But when life throws so much at you all at once, when do you find time to serve? This is where prayer comes in. God will help you in all your righteous desires. He wants to bless you, especially when you want to help others. Sometimes all it takes is a simple prayer to unlock miracles and to open your mind to how you can help people in need. It's a wonderful thing. With consistent prayer and scripture study over a long period of time, you will see miracles unfold in your life.

Why would I say over a long period of time? One thing I have noticed is spiritual and physical things are opposite yet the same—like mirror images. If my theory is true and you want to see physical improvement, you need to develop a physical habit over a period of time. For example, losing twenty pounds in a healthy way may take three or four months of consistent working out and eating clean. You start to see results *over time*. It's much in the same way with your spirit. With consistent prayer and scripture study over a long period of time, you start to see the will of God unfold in your life and you will feel spiritual growth.

If prayer and scripture study are so good, why do we need to go to church? I was having this conversation with a neighbor who lived across the street. He believed in God but had no spiritual structure in his life and didn't see the need for organized religion. He believed spiritual growth was a personal thing and something you could do on your own. We did have one common belief—we both agreed service and helping others was essential to spiritual growth. I mentioned how my church offered many different opportunities to serve. He said he could find his own ways to serve and that he didn't need an organization to find opportunities to help others.

Funny thing though—the week before our conversation, there was a terrible windstorm that came through the area and knocked down a tree in his neighbor's yard. It was right behind his house; they shared a fence. There was no serious damage, but the owner of the house was a sweet elderly lady who had no business removing a tree from her backyard. She also didn't have the money to have it removed professionally. At the time, I was a leader in my church's young men's program. When they made the announcement about the fallen tree at church, it was my job to rally the young men. Meanwhile, the adult men were gathering their chainsaws, tools, and trailers.

The conversation I had with my neighbor helped me understand the importance of belonging to a church community. Only a nonprofit service organization could have pulled that many people and that much equipment together to get the job done quickly and efficiently. My friend, who lived right behind the sweet old lady, had no idea she had a fallen tree in her yard. And if he had known and wanted to help, he would not have had the manpower to get the job done fast. Sure, he could have done it all by himself, but it would have taken him days or even weeks. That conversation and service project helped me realize how being an active part of an organization that focuses on service is key to spiritual growth.

Why is service so key to becoming a spiritual person? Isn't there another way to become spiritual? Trust me, I've heard it all, and no, there really isn't. Why?

When I was a Scout leader, the boys would always whine when they heard the phrase "service project." "Why, why, why?" they would ask. "All we ever do is service projects!"

I'm not too proud to admit I personally have had a hard time with the nature of service projects on occasion. Serving others sometimes puts my life and my goals on hold and interferes with my personal agenda. And yet, though service may not be the most fun or convenient thing we can do, I do believe our spiritual journey must revolve around service or helping others.

Chapter 5
Spiritual and Physical Growth

To understand why spiritual growth revolves around service, we must understand the difference between the spirit and the body. Are they different or one and the same? Do we even have a spirit? Let me ask: Do you have a physical body? Of course. We can prove that using our physical senses. It is not just based on evidence; we can prove over and over that we have a body. We need proof to verify that something exists, right? So how do we know we have a spirit? When it comes to our spirit, we can't prove it exists, but we can collect evidence.

What would that spiritual evidence look like? First, we have to know what we are looking for to collect evidence, so we need a definition. We need to define *spirit*. The dictionary tells us it is a "vital force, immortal part of man or ghost." So, is there an essential, immortal, life-giving force within all of us? Is there a part of us that lives on after we die? The answer becomes evident as we begin to understand the difference between body and spirit.

The body is physical. It requires nutrients from the earth to grow and exist; when we die, it will go back to the earth. Our bodies have built-in instincts; instincts are the habits we are preprogrammed with to ensure the best odds for our survival. Our instincts are not much different from the instincts of animals. Like animals, we need food, water, and shelter. That takes care of our individual survival, but now we must ensure the survival of future generations through reproduction. The physical body is selfish—until after reproduction. Once a baby is born, the parents now have to ensure survival for themselves and their offspring.

Animals have developed behaviors that ensure the best odds for their survival. There are always exceptions, but for the most part, their behaviors are predictable. What about humans? If you look at predictable behaviors, then yes, we all have a few. But all it takes is a quick look around to see that humans do some things that don't always make sense—things that have nothing to do with survival. It goes both ways: we engage in unpredictable good behaviors and unpredictable bad behaviors that have nothing to do with survival. Do these good and bad behaviors allude to the fact that we have a spirit dictating our behavior? If you look at the good side of humanity, there are instances where we can see an inexplicable human behavior that has nothing to do with survival. One of the first that comes to mind is the assisted-living facility for seniors. My wife is a caregiver at one, and I often hear the sad stories of families who can't afford to keep their loved ones in assisted living and also don't have the time to take care of them.

When it comes to survival of the species, we technically don't need senior citizens if they can't reproduce or work. What do they contribute to humankind's survival? Nothing. I know that sounds harsh, but bear with me—I think you will see my point. They don't help us build, eat, or survive in any way. As a matter fact, quite the opposite. If you have ever spent time around a senior citizen who is not self-sufficient, you know the burden often placed on loved ones.

Of course, we love and respect our parents and grandparents and want to keep them happy and comfortable in their final years. Our devotion to them is readily apparent. You can see this in the way we go to great financial lengths to keep them with us. If they can't walk, we give them wheelchairs. When they become bedridden, we make sure they are fed and comfortable throughout their final days. We keep them breathing with oxygen tanks and nourished by hand-feeding them pureed food. Where does this love for parents and grandparents come from? Some see it as a chance to pay them back. Others say it is because these senior citizens have experience and knowledge they can share with us.

So let me ask—why do we shelter and feed the homeless when they are not willing to work? And why do we allow repeat criminal offenders back into society? When I see the mercy we extend to senior citizens, the homeless, criminals, and others who can't survive independently, my heart is filled with joy. It's amazing how willing people are to help and forgive even when it creates a burden in their life. Is our willingness to help those who may be a burden to us evidence that we have an enlightened thought process motivated by a spirit? It's certainly not instinctual as far as survival.

Now let's take a look at the animal kingdom and see how lions deal with the elderly lions in their pride. Once a young male is large enough to challenge the alpha male, he does so. If the young male wins the fight, he becomes the new king of the jungle, as they say. Being the new alpha male, he has breeding rights with the whole pride. And what of the old king? He is banished and left to survive on his own, and he's usually been injured in that final battle. One more interesting fact: normally, female lions are better hunters than the males. Lions hunt in packs, so being injured, old, and banished from the pride, the old king's days are numbered. But there is no shame in his death. The cycle of life has run its course, he no longer offers his species any value, and it's his time to die. One more interesting yet gruesome fact about lions: the new alpha male can't breed with females who already have cubs. These females have no interest in mating when they already have cubs to care for. The most important thing to the new alpha is his own brood. The existing cubs born of the old king have no value to him. The simple solution for this guy is to get rid of the existing cubs so the females will breed with him. How would a lion get rid of cubs? By eating them. It brings new light to the term *dinner and date*. The crazy thing is the females just go ahead and breed with the blood-thirsty male as if it's no big deal. All this is a testament to the importance of instinctual survival in the wild.

In so many instances in the animal kingdom, survival for yourself and your posterity is the only goal. Even animals playing is an instinct developed to help young animals adapt to their social structure and environment. It's easy to see that in the animal kingdom, survival using any means possible is the name of the game.

Inexplicable Human Behavior

Why do humans exhibit such inexplicable behavior? Could it be that the acts of kindness we perform is evidence that we have a higher level of intelligence, aka a spirit? Is taking care of the poor and needy a spiritual behavior that indicates our spiritual nature?

We humans also engage in behaviors completely counterproductive to the survival of the species. For example, some use dangerous substances such as illegal drugs. We see the effects drug abuse has, and we do our best to teach our children that these harmful substances can ruin their lives. Yet people still experiment with them, even when there is no productive use for them as far as human survival is concerned, and, in fact, quite the opposite. Humans have survived for thousands of years without these drugs.

As a fighter, I'm no stranger to painkillers. I've been operated on five times due to sports injuries. I've used prescription drugs. They are great, and I'm so thankful for them. But being addicted to illegal drugs is devastating to human productivity. Then why, no matter how well we educate our children, do we still have drug problems? And, yes, animals can be addicted to drugs as well, but the difference is that animals, such as rats and mice, are forced to take the drugs and have no idea they are addictive or lethal. We take harmful substances even when we know they can kill us. When all other species are obsessed with survival, why is it we are so captivated with self-corruption through substance abuse or even self-destruction through suicide?

Humans have also developed strange sexual behaviors that do us no good. We commit awful crimes that make no sense concerning our survival. If a higher life form were to do a documentary on the human race explaining our behavior, they would likely be stumped. Why do we engage in behaviors for both good and evil that make no sense when it comes to our survival?

If these unexplained acts of good and evil are evidence that our spirits exist, could it be that our spirits are what influence the decision-making process? Does a kind, caring spirit motivate us to altruistically help and care for others? Does an evil spirit influence us to behave in a way that not only doesn't benefit the human cause but undermines it? Why is it that humans are so extreme in their behavior? Could it be that our behaviors are dictated by our spirit? And do our spirits define who we are as people? Sure you could make a counterargument to the evidence of inexplicable human behavior, but that's just because all it is evidence, not proof.

Learning without Being Taught?

The next piece of evidence is the ability to learn without being taught or without instinct to guide us. When I think of people like Sir Isaac Newton, Antoine Lavoisier, Michael Faraday, or Albert Einstein, I can't imagine what it would have been like to acquire the knowledge they did without first being taught the laws they discovered. I try to understand some of the laws of physics, and I struggle. Even with teaching tools such as videos, books, and teachers, I don't feel I truly understand much of what these great minds discovered. Learning without being taught—how is that possible? Could it be that our minds can at times jump to a higher plane of understanding through spiritual intervention? Or is it that during these times of higher understanding our spirits are having a physical intervention with our bodies? Whatever the case, we continue to make great leaps in understanding our universe. It always make me wonder if human discovery is also evidence that we have spirits and if our spirits intervene with our conscious thought process.

If we all have a spirit, it seems there are different degrees of human existence that dictate our behavior:

First Degree

The spirit controls the body, and if it's a good spirit, it works to help others and spends its time in acts of service.

Second Degree

The body controls the spirit; this would be a life full of selfish acts. The body has needs and wants, and this kind of person works and spends their time trying to gratify their own selfish desires. Basically, this type of person acts without regard for the needs of others.

Third Degree

The spirit controls the body, and if it's an evil spirit, it will work to hurt others and spend its time in committing acts of terror.

We began this chapter talking about how spiritual growth revolves around service. It's because if we have a spirit, we strengthen that spirit through our actions. The power the spirit gains through action is discovery and knowledge. Extreme behavior in service or extreme behavior in terror promotes discovery and knowledge. Our actions define what we are in this life and what our spirit will become in preparation for the next life. If love and service are what define you and your actions, you have lifted the cross and work for Christ. If acts of terror define you, you are a tool in the hands of the devil.

The beauty of it is that because we have a spirit, we have a choice. We can take power from the spirit and give it to the body. If we give power to the body, we are in the second degree of existence. In this type of existence, we act like animals by chasing our needs and wants. Or we can take power from the body and give it to the spirit. Now we must decide what type of spirit we want dictating our actions. The spirit is a powerful force for comprehension and understanding. If we choose acts of terror (the third degree), our spirit will find ways to bring pain and suffering to others. It's no wonder wartime has historically been a time of revolution and technological advancement. In these times of extreme behavior, powerful minds and spirits on both sides of the coin are inspired to bring forth methods to ensure their success.

Most people I know want to be good. If your goal is to be a good, helpful person, that puts you in the first degree of existence—you want to strengthen your spirit in good ways. The way you strengthen that good spirit is by doing good things over a long period of time. Physical and spiritual growth work in a similar fashion. Long periods of consistent behavior enable the body and spirit to progress in either a good or bad direction.

If you want to experience positive spiritual growth, you must involve yourself in acts of service and in helping others over a long period of time.

So what does spiritual growth have to do with fighting? Instinct is something humans and animals have in common. If you live by instinct alone, you exist on the same plane as animals, or within the second degree of existence, doing only that which you are programed to do to survive. One example of instinctual behavior is when fighters spar for the first time. We all have either a fight or flight instinct.

Those with a flight instinct will reach straight out in front of them and pull their head as far back as possible at the first sign of danger, creating a huge gap between the head and their only line of defense—their hands. Their legs stiffen, and they start to move backward, which is the worst thing a fighter can do because it almost always puts them against the ropes. And being cornered is an awful place to be.

When those with a fight instinct spar for the first time, they walk forward in a straight line, constantly throwing punches, with no regard for danger, which is also a terrible place to be. Often those with a fight-only attitude completely forget about defense. I have seen so many people get knocked out when they push forward; all their opponent has to do is step back, change angles, then attack.

That is what makes fighting an art. It is a game of chess while you are under stress, in pain, and strategically trying to best your opponent.

Fighting is a lot like life. If you fight only on instinct, whether flight or fight, you will never get any better. The key to becoming a great fighter is to stay humble, recognize the habits that are hurting you, work every day to change those habits, then work every day to develop habits that will help you fight better.

In both fighting and life, you must rise above that which you were born with and work hard to become better than you were yesterday.

Chapter 6
Fight Principles

As a fighter, there are principles you must follow to ensure success. Fighting is no more than a mathematical formula. You are constantly calculating all your movements versus all your opponent's movements. It always comes down to statistics, odds, and probabilities. In a fight, you always want the odds to fall in your favor.

Let's start with the basics. Be on your toes. Why? If you are on your toes, you can move more efficiently, and more efficient movement means you can better avoid damage and also better deliver damage.

Now let's use our "be-on-your-toes" formula in a stand-up fight. We have two fighters who are equally matched, are in the same weight class, and have similar fighting experience. If they fight for fifteen minutes, and fighter A was on his toes for twelve minutes and fighter B was on his toes for only eight minutes, based on the principle of being on your toes to avoid damage and deliver damage a majority of the time, who wins the fight?

If the formula holds true, fighter A wins most of the time. I say A wins *most* of the time because there are so many variables in a fight, you can't always predict every outcome. But you can develop habits that give you a higher probability of winning. We talked about one basic formula—staying on your toes. Here are a few more habits you need to develop as a fighter:

1. Be on your toes.
2. Have your hands up.

3. Move your head.
4. Move your feet.

If you think about these techniques, none of them actually win the fight. It's normally punching and kicking that wins the fight. But being on your toes, having your hands up, moving your head, and moving your feet all keep you safe and put you in a position to land punches and kicks.

If you think of fighting as a mathematical formula, it seems simple. Perfect these techniques and you become a perfect fighter. And as a perfect fighter, no one should be able to beat you. It's easy; just be perfect. Right?

In the gym I refer to a principle called "levels of perfection." People have moments of perfection in different ways. You can be perfect while shadow boxing in the mirror. Next, you perfect those same movements while hitting the punching bag. Then, you perfect those movements while hitting mitts with your coach. After that, you continue perfecting the technique while sparring. These moments of perfection lead to perfection in a real fight.

Just be perfect—it sounds simple enough. It isn't. Being imperfect is part of being human: no one is perfect. We can all work hard and have moments of perfection, but no one is perfect. We all make mistakes. Even the best fighters in the world get hit and lose fights.

If these habits become a priority in your training, you are on track to becoming a great fighter. But no matter how hard you work and no matter how good you get as a fighter, you will never be perfect; if you fight long enough, you will get hit and lose. One thing I have learned from fighting is that no one is perfect. With hard work we can improve, but we can never be perfect—*ever*.

Nothing can convince me otherwise. Humans make a lot of mistakes—both in combat sports and in life. We talked earlier about gaining a relationship with God through talking with Him in prayer. I also mentioned service and aligning ourselves with others who are trying to find God using similar habits. The reason I bring up our imperfections is to point out a few things you can experiment with as you fight to find God.

Here are some facts I know are true:

Humans are far from perfect, meaning we all make mistakes. It is our imperfect, selfish nature that separates us from our all-powerful, perfect Creator. The phrase "Birds of a feather flock together" illustrates my point: God can't allow us to dwell with Him when we are so different from Him. In the Pearl of Great Price, God says, "For behold, this is my work and my glory—to bring to pass the immortality and eternal life of man" (Moses 1:39). That is what God is all about: bringing eternal life to mankind. That's it—His goal is to glorify us, His children, through His plan. As we live our lives and chase our selfish desires, we constantly separate ourselves from God. Our agenda is not the same as His agenda. As we fail to align our lives with God's will, we disqualify ourselves from being in His presence. We become birds of a different feather.

God is perfect. He is Perfect in power and dominion over all things both spiritual and physical. He is also perfect in action, motivation, and love. And He has a perfect understanding and application of justice and mercy.

Why are these defining words for God important? When we define God's attributes, we start to see his plan unfold. For instance, let's look at the last sentence in the previous paragraph. "God has a perfect understanding and application of justice and mercy." It is justice that keeps us separated from God and His eternal joy. We have not *earned* the right to be in His all-powerful, peaceful, glorified presence, and we never will. Being in His presence comes at a price. It would be unjust to allow us—imperfect sinners—to feel the glory and power of our perfect God. Mercy is the fact that God has provided a way for us to live with Him again.

Many have asked me, "If God is so powerful, why can't He just bring us to Him? Then we could skip out on all the difficult stuff, like the pain we feel throughout life. Why can't He just *make* us perfect like Him? I mean, if God really loves us and is all-powerful, can't He just make us perfect?"

I've coached a fight team for the last five years, and there is a standard each fighter must maintain to be on our team. There are two main requirements: First, fighters must spar one hundred rounds in the gym with a coach present. Second, they must provide a handwritten copy of our basic grappling system. It is nine pages and includes fifty-four different wrestling moves. I require this because I want fighters taking notes during class. Once it's written, it must be memorized. And only when it's written and memorized is the fighter allowed to take the test. In the test, the fighter demonstrates the fifty-four moves without notes in front of the class. It's the fight team who votes and declares whether or not the candidate has passed. The average fighter will fail the test twice before they finally succeed on the third try. Usually, it takes a dedicated fighter about six months to become a member of our fight team. I developed the program to make sure the fighters are ready for their first fight. What makes our team unique is that you need to be a dedicated fighter to earn a spot. When you struggle, have a high probability of failure, and overcome the challenge, the sense of achievement you experience is far greater than if something were just handed to you. As I think about our fight team, I see the purpose of struggling throughout life.

Do you need to earn your way into God's kingdom? In God's plan there is no way you can succeed on our own. There is no amount of perfection you can ever obtain that will qualify you to be in His presence. You have already created a separation from God through your selfish actions. Don't feel bad. It's not just you. It's everyone. We are all born lost and with many carnal desires. So even if you obtained perfection today, it would still not justify you to be in God's presence due to the debt you have already acquired through your previous mistakes. So to be reunited with our Creator, we need to be perfect from now on and also repay the debt we have acquired through our previous selfish actions.

Throughout my experiences as a coach and athlete, I've become convinced it is not possible for humans to obtain perfection; that's what makes us human. Being imperfect in all things divides us from God. He gave us a perfect soul when we were born, and we corrupted it. We were all perfectly innocent as babies, but we corrupted that innocence through continually making mistakes. Simply put, we cannot be perfect. It's not possible. Even if we could be perfect from now on, it would not be enough to save us from our previous mistakes.

God's power and perfection in all things and our constant failure in all things is what divides us from Him. So how is it possible for us to have these special moments of spirit-to-spirit communication with God despite these differences? We can have spirit-to-spirit communication with God because of His perfect love and mercy. He is perfect in power and dominion over all things both spiritual and physical. He is also perfect in action, motivation, and love and has a perfect understanding and application of justice and mercy.

Yes, that's right—perfect in love and mercy. What does that mean? He loves all of us because we are His creation. How can He be perfect in mercy? Because of God's perfect love and mercy, He's provided a plan that allows us to return to Him again someday despite our mistakes and differences.

God is perfect and has power and dominion over all things both spiritual and physical combined. His perfect understanding and application of justice and mercy necessitated a Savior.

What is a Savior? Since we separate ourselves from God through sin, He needed a man capable of coming to earth; this man needed to be perfect. But perfection itself was not enough. A perfect life would only qualify the perfect man to return to live with God. But God wanted all of us back, not just one of us. The one perfect man needed to be perfect Himself so he could make up the difference for all who have sinned. It seems unimaginable—to be perfect personally and bring everyone else up to godly perfection as well. How is it possible? It all started before the world was. God, the Father of all creation, created all things spiritually before He created them physically. That means you, me, and every living thing—all were created spiritually before we were created physically.

That is how we became our Father's spirit children. In the time of spiritual creation, there was one who was far beyond all others and was like God and who became God's Only Begotten in perfection and exact likeness. In the premortal existence, this perfect begotten spirit was qualified to take upon Himself godly responsibilities and do exactly what God would do in all things, and that was be perfect unto God in all things. This perfect spirit child became so aligned with God it was as if He and God became one—one in purpose though different in existence. God was spiritual and physical, having power over all things spiritual and physical. God's spiritually perfect Begotten Son only had power spiritually because that's all He was; He was spirit only, not yet having received a body. However, His alignment with God was so exact that God granted Him power over physical things because He had the same desires as God. All the things God wanted, His perfect Begotten Son wanted also, and so it was done. God and His perfect spirit child were one and the same, yet two separate perfect beings.

When it came to creating the heavens and the earth, God allowed this perfect spirit child to create the heavens and the earth exactly as God Himself would have created them. So who created the heavens and the earth, God or His Son? It was God. How can that be? Because it was God's power and authority given to His Son to act in God's name in creating the heavens and the earth. That means God's spiritual Son created the heavens and the earth in God's name exactly as God Himself would have done it. And so all things were made in their physical form by God's perfect Son, and God's Son became God over all the earth.

In the English translation of the King James version of the Bible, God's Son is known as Jehovah. Jehovah is translated from the Hebrew word *YHWH*, pronounced "Yahweh." God and Jehovah have been called many different names throughout time. As you read this book, the important thing to remember is that when I use the term *God*, I'm talking about the Father of all things spiritual and physical. When I use the term *Jehovah*, I'm talking about His Son, who was given authority to create all things physical.

In the Old Testament, Jehovah demonstrated His power over all things physical in creating the heavens and the earth. He did this for God's spirit children so that each of us could have a place to live while in our physical body. Jehovah was the God of Adam and Eve. He was also the same God who flooded the earth in the time of Noah to save the righteous from the wicked. He also destroyed Sodom and Gomorrah in the time of Abraham so His covenant people would not be oppressed by worldly power. Then, in Moses' day, Jehovah saved His covenant people from slavery through pestilence. Later, it was Jehovah who worked through Moses in dividing the Red Sea so the children of Israel could flee Egypt on dry ground. It was Jehovah, God's perfect Son, who performed all of these miracles throughout the Old Testament, showing His absolute power, authority, and dominion over the earth.

In New Testament times, it was Jehovah who took on a physical body and came to earth as an infant, just like every other person. But this was no ordinary infant. His mother, Mary, was a virgin. Jehovah was brought to Mary by the hand of His Father, God. Being born of a mortal made Him mortal, but having a Father who was eternal gave Him power beyond comprehension. It was this power that gave Him the ability not only to be perfect but also to pay the price for our sins.

The infant born to Mary in Bethlehem is known today as Jesus Christ. The name Jesus was given Him from his mortal father, Joseph, as directed by the angel Gabriel at His circumcision. And we learn from LDS.org that "Jesus is called the *Christ* (a Greek word) or the *Messiah* (an Aramaic word). Both words mean "the anointed." He is the one *anointed* of the Father to be the Father's personal representative in all things pertaining to the salvation of mankind."

Jesus Christ is also known by many other titles. A few I have mentioned, such as Creator, Jehovah, and Savior. We see names given to Christ based on things He has done, is doing, or will do. Prophets before His birth foretold of the coming Christ child, and many followers after His death have preached of His magnificence to this very day. As we look at the names given Him by great prophets and faithful followers, we can see how these titles define His power and glory. Below is a list of names for Christ, and while it is a long list, it's worth noting the way in which each name characterizes who He is.

Jesus Christ, Shiloh, Emmanuel, Lord, Wonderful, Emanuel, Counselor, Mighty God, Prince of Peace, Everlasting Father, Stem of Jesse, Mighty One of Jacob, Righteousness, Messiah, Messenger, Redeemer, Holy One, Blessed of God, Son of David, Son of Abraham, Joseph's Son, the Carpenter's Son, the Carpenter, Jesus of Galilee, Jesus of Nazareth, Nazarene, Beloved Son of God, Only Begotten, One with the Father, the Lord's Christ, Chosen of God, the Lamb of God, the King, Meek and Lowly, the King of the Jews, Governor, King of Israel, King of Sion, Consolation of Israel, Savior of the World, Lord of All, Rabbi, Rabboni, the Word, the Light, Living Bread, Living Water, Light of the World, the Good Shepherd, Resurrection and the Life, the Truth, the Way, the Life, the Just, Prince of Life, Judge, I Am, Deliverer, Alpha and Omega, Beginning and End, Minister, the Rock, the Express Image of God, God Manifest in the Flesh, Son of Man, Chief Cornerstone, Foundation of the Church, Head of the Church, Right Hand of God, Mediator, God Manifest in the Flesh, Heir of all Things, Purged our Sin, Key of David, the Lion of Judah, the Morning Star, Brother, Son, and Savior.

Let's take a look at a few of these names, starting with Savior. What exactly is a savior? It is someone who saves or rescues. Jesus Christ saves, or rescues, us from sin, and sin is what separates us from God.

How does Christ save us from sin? Christ qualified Himself for the responsibility of saving our souls in the very beginning by being one with God. As mentioned, He was a perfect likeness of God in desire, motivation, willingness, and love. Thus we see the name given Him of the Express Image of God or God Manifest in the Flesh. God Himself is perfect in body and spirit, which means God has eternal life physically and spiritually. He is immortal. Because His body and spirit were sealed for eternity, God's immortal nature disqualified God from becoming our Savior. God is our Creator, yes, but the saving grace necessary for saving our souls required one who could take on a mortal body and suffer all the pains the world has to offer. Why did it have to be Jesus? Because Jesus is a god; he has all of God's power in Him. His godly power qualified and allowed Him to suffer all the pain the world has ever experienced and will ever experience.

Christ was already qualified to be in God's presence before He came to the earth, and He had power over all things physical through His Father. Christ's alignment with God in all things allowed Him eternal life with God. As fallible human beings, we can offer Christ nothing. His election to eternal glory was sealed upon Him from the beginning. It's humbling to know Christ would come to earth and suffer for us when He was already sealed to God through His perfect alignment with Him. Christ did come to earth, and He did prove His perfection in all things while in a mortal body. As I understand who Christ really is, I see how insignificant I am when it comes to perfection and power. Moses said it best in the Pearl of Great Price: "Now, for this cause I know that man is nothing, which thing I never had supposed" (Moses 1:10). If you think about it, without the Lord and His sacrifice, we really are nothing. Without Him, when we die, we would cease to exist, our body going back to the earth to rise no more.

Once again, how is it possible to have spirit-to-spirit moments with God if God and His glory are so far beyond our nothingness? The answer to the question is Jesus Christ! One of the names given to Christ is Mediator. Christ is our go-between. He bridged the gap between us and God when he took upon Himself a mortal body as a God and then condescended to experience physical humiliation and take upon Himself the sins of the world. As Christ entered the Garden of Gethsemane, He felt the weight of the world. Christ's godly lineage qualified Him to feel all the pain this world has offered and ever will offer. Every sin the world has committed has already been rectified—past, present, and future—in what is known as the Atonement. The weight of our sins pained His soul to the point that His pain justified each of us to be in God's presence. While on earth, Christ was willing to suffer physical and spiritual pain even though He was spiritually the God of all the earth under His Father's direction, which qualified Him to become the Mediator, which in turn meant that Christ could cleanse our souls and qualify us to feel His and God's presence. We are qualified to receive a body and obtain eternal life because Christ was willing to take upon Himself a body and suffer for our sins. If you are trying to find God, you can do that through Christ.

If you are not sure about the need for a Savior, ask God if a Savior is necessary. Ask Him now. Put down this book and ask Him if you need a Savior. And ask God if Christ is your Savior. Ask Him if Jesus Christ is the reason this world exists. Ask Him if Christ is the means by which we can communicate with God. Once again, allow God to be God as you think about the necessity of a Savior. Ask yourself if Christ is the reason God's plan works. Then listen and wait for God to communicate with you, and open your mind to all the possibilities. Please do not move on to the next chapter until you have asked God these questions in prayer.

Chapter 7
How Does Your Corner Affect the Fight?

I'VE INVITED YOU TO PRAY twice now. If you are unsure how God answers prayers, this chapter will shed light on that concept. One thing you need to remember as you communicate with God is to pay attention to how you feel and the thoughts that come to your mind. Also during this chapter, pay attention to your thoughts and feelings regarding the Holy Ghost as I explain the Holy Ghost.

It's time to look at another fighting–finding God comparison.

Before a wrestling match begins, both contestants are given an ankle band—one a red band, the other a green band. At the end of the first round, the referee flips a coin with a red and green side. The winner of the coin toss gets to choose top, bottom, neutral, or to defer. If you choose top, you literally get to start the next round on top of your opponent. If you choose bottom, you start the next round on bottom. Choosing neutral means you and your opponent start on your feet. If you defer, you let your opponent choose top, bottom, or neutral. By deferring between the first and second rounds, you get to choose top, bottom, or neutral between the second and third rounds.

During my junior high wrestling matches, between the first and second rounds when I won the coin toss, the referee would ask me if I wanted top, bottom, neutral, or to defer. If my opponent won the coin toss and he deferred, the referee would ask if I wanted top, bottom, or neutral. It was in these moments I looked to my coach.

While this may seem like a simple question, it was not for this young, adrenaline-filled wrestler. With all the confusion I experienced during a match, I always found comfort in knowing that my coach had the experience necessary to give me the right answer. Many new wrestlers think you should pick top because you would naturally have the advantage. But that's not always the case. You can actually score more points from bottom by escaping than getting the takedown. However, if you feel your opponent is better than you are, you definitely don't want to start with him on top and risk getting pinned. A lot goes into making the best decision between rounds, and having a coach who is calm, cool, and collected helping you make those decisions is comforting. That is one way having a coach in your corner helps you get the most out of every match.

I have been cornering and coaching fights for years. I cornered my first MMA fight when I was eighteen years old. I've also coached junior high wrestling, freestyle and Greco wrestling for all ages, and jiu-jitsu for eight years with a team that traveled all over to compete. At one time I even trained MMA fighters out of my garage.

In 2013 I opened my gym, Factum MMA. My business partner, Phil, and I hired Tim, our boxing instructor. Tim became our head boxing coach. I was the head MMA coach. However, I often assist Tim with the boxing team, and Tim often assists me with the MMA team. Between boxing, jiu-jitsu, and MMA, it seems we are coaching and cornering events every other weekend. Some months it seems we have events going on every weekend. There have been weekends when we coach boxing bouts Friday night and then MMA fights on Saturday. I've fought, cornered, and coached at numerous events.

One thing many new fighters have told me is how, during a fight, they are surprised they can distinctly hear my voice. If you think about the situation, it really is surprising they can hear me over the crowd, which can at times be deafening. This is not due to my voice being distinct or loud; it's because in the midst of competition, you subconsciously tune in to those you know and trust.

It has happened to me on many different occasions. One time I was boxing in Wendover, Utah. It was the third round, and I was running out of gas fast. I wasn't even sure I was going to be able to finish the fight. I had been winning up to that point, but I was starting to worry I would get knocked out in the last round because I could not bring my hands up to my face to defend myself. I knew I needed to pick up my hands, but I physically could not do it. Then I heard Tim's voice. "Two, three, two!" Straight, hook, straight.

I knew I would not be able to knock my opponent out, but I thought throwing something was better than standing there with my hands down and doing nothing. So I threw a weak and slow two, three, two, but it landed. It was far too weak to knock him out or even hurt him, but it gave me the confidence I needed to keep throwing punches. And I kept punching until the round was over. I didn't knock him out, but I did win the fight on the judges' scorecard due to my newfound ability to keep punching when I didn't think I would be able to. I kept punching because a wise coach knew what combo to yell. He inspired me to throw the right punch even though it was weak. But it was enough to keep me moving in the right direction and to ensure the win.

During these long, grueling fights, coaches become an absolute necessity. The longer and more difficult the fight, the more important your corner becomes.

Let's talk about a fight and what it's like in a long hand-to-hand combat situation. First, the buildup to the fight is awful. A few days before the fight, it's constant nerves, and it seems there's nothing you can do to make those nerves go away. On the day of the fight, they continue to build at the event center as you see other fighters warming up and talking strategy with their teammates. Some fighters seclude themselves, and some get loud and try to make conversation and joke around in an attempt to make the nerves go away.

When you walk toward the cage to the sound of your fight song, the nervousness is amplified. Sometimes the crowd gives you a big welcoming cheer; other times, if your opponent has a lot of fans, you walk out to people booing and yelling hateful things at you. The booing only makes the situation more intense as you try to relax and think about your game plan. Then, your corner preps you, making sure you have a cup, mouthpiece, and Vaseline for your face to help you avoid getting cut during the fight. Lastly, your corner gives you a few quick words of advice and encouragement.

When I step into the cage, I always notice how cold and hard the steel steps are against my bare feet. Then, I notice the contrast of the exceptionally soft mats in the cage. The mats in the cage are always softer than the mats we practice on. I have trained in many gyms, and actual fight mats are always softer. The other thing I notice is how the mats in the cage are always dirty. I feel the dirt and grime on my feet. It's normal to see blood on the mat—usually from a previous fight that night.

If I am called out second, I always approach my opponent and offer a handshake. If I am called out first, I offer my hand as well. Most the time, I see relief in his eyes as I offer a greeting. The acknowledgment stands as a symbol of appreciation and gratitude and brings a feeling of comfort. We realize we are not fighting because we hate each other; we are fighting because the fight stands as a benchmark of how we are achieving our goals.

But there have been fights when an opponent will not shake my hand. When that happens, it shows me the fight is personal for him, that there is an element of hate, and that fighting is a way for him to satisfy his need for violence. It is not an act of personal progression for him. Whichever the case, the official brings us to the center, has a few short words with us regarding rules, and asks if we have any questions. Once he sends us back to our opposite sides, he points to each of us and asks if we are ready. If both fighters nod, the official says something like "Let's get it on."

It's amazing to me how the nerves go away when the fight starts. It's as if the entire world falls away and the only thing left standing is the cage, you, and your opponent. Though the nerves are gone, the fear of being hit is still real—until you get hit. It's mind-boggling when you get hit for the first time in a fight and realize that it did not hurt. Yes that's right—getting hit in a fight does not hurt. It affects your ability to fight by reducing your energy and restricting your movements, but in terms of actual pain—not really. It's rare to hear a fighter cry out in pain during a fight. I have seen fighters acknowledge a broken hand between rounds, but they state it matter-of-factly, not as a cry for sympathy. Regardless of the injury—a cut, broken bone, or dislocated joint—you don't normally see fighters show pain until after the fight.

Some may question whether a fight is really that grueling if there is no pain. Let me explain. Fighting is a lot like drowning if you are losing, and swimming if you are winning. If you don't feel panicked, you are probably doing fine, but you must keep working because swimming can turn into drowning in a split second. The key is to not panic. You may or may not be winning, but if you have a cool head, you've won half the battle already. If you are not panicked, you are at least giving yourself a chance to win.

The pressure of a fight becomes almost too much if you are stubborn and determined to win at all costs. As you and your opponent battle it out, you are forced to dig deep and to push your body far beyond what is normal. The agony I feel during a fight is not isolated to one part of my body due to a strike. It's more of a burn that starts in my lungs and radiates out through my shoulders. This pain is often so excruciating that even though I know I need to be on my toes, I can't do it. I know I need my hands in front of my face, but I just can't seem to get them up. The pain in my lungs becomes so overwhelming I can't move properly or think straight. It's this burning in my lungs that reminds me of drowning. It is an awful feeling during a fight when no matter how hard I breathe, I can't seem to get enough oxygen. Without enough oxygen, my body starts to give up, and then my survival instinct becomes more important than winning. It is an actual feeling of suffocation I experience during a long, hard fight. And if I have taken a few hits to the body or face, it seriously affects my abilities even though, like I said, the actual strike does not hurt.

One time in a fight, I took a direct jab, then a cross to the face. In that moment, the punches did not hurt, but I remember the world becoming distant and thinking I would not be able to win that fight. I could barely stand up. Even taking simple steps became almost impossible. That's common when I've been hit in the face.

If your opponent hits you with a solid body shot, your breathing can be knocked out of whack and you begin to feel like you're suffocating. If it doesn't end the fight, it can most definitely lead to a sense of panic and thoughts of quitting. I experienced this once when one of my ribs separated from my sternum and I was unable to move my torso. Once I realized I could not properly move from my waist up to my shoulders, I knew I had lost. We fought a bit longer, but I was not at full capacity and was relieved when my opponent put me in a choke hold. It is embarrassing to admit, but when your body becomes debilitated, you sometimes resort to humiliating things like letting someone choke you out.

I have also been cut many times during fights. The first time I got cut, I remember seeing blood on my opponent first. It was on him because I was on top and *my* blood was dripping down on him. As we got back up on our feet, I discovered we were both covered in blood, but I didn't know where the blood was coming from. I hoped it was his; I hate getting stitches. Then I tasted the blood in my mouth. At that moment my thoughts completely flip-flopped. I hoped it *was* my blood, otherwise it meant I had his blood in my mouth.

And let's not forget the fear of losing. Even if you're winning, if the fight is not over, there's still a chance you will lose, so the fear and anxiety of losing don't go away until the fight has been called and is officially over.

I have lost games in many different sports, but losing an MMA fight is the worst. It hurts more than anything, both physically and mentally, because your ego is directly attached to your ability to fight. If you lose a fight, your ego takes a direct hit because there's no one else to blame but yourself.

There are times where a fighter experiences a mental and physical breakdown and there is only one source of strength to turn to. It is your corner's job to help you keep your head in the game when the fight becomes unbearable. Your corner becomes a comfort, encouraging you to fight harder and giving you advice that can help you win. Knowing firsthand the agony a fighter experiences, I can tell you that a fighter most definitely needs a corner. If given the choice to fight with or without a corner, there is no question: I will always choose to fight with a corner on my side.

We have a similar support in this fight called life. God has given us an option to live with or without a corner—the Holy Ghost. What exactly is Holy Ghost? In the various Christian religions, we hear the phrase "Father, Son, and the Holy Ghost." We've talked about God as our spiritual Father and about His Son, Jesus Christ. But where does the Holy Ghost fit in? Who is the Holy Ghost, and what is His relationship to us?

Let's recap what we've said about God and Christ so we can see how the Holy Ghost fits in and how His relationship falls in line with the Father and the Son. Remember, God is the *eternal* Creator. He created all things *spiritually*. He also created a plan that gives us the opportunity to live with Him again someday. In this plan, the Son was qualified to create us *physically* because he was in total alignment with and consequently represented the Father. Then, the Son became Jehovah, who took on a mortal body and is known to us today as Jesus Christ. Jehovah became a man, yet was still a God. Jehovah became Jesus Christ. His godly nature qualified Him to suffer through the Atonement, the act wherein Christ suffered and died for our sins. Our all-powerful Savior also demonstrated perfect humility during the Crucifixion. Suffering through the Atonement and allowing Himself to be crucified qualified Him to pay the price for our sins spiritually and perfect our bodies physically.

In God's plan, the Father and the Son have done Their part. They have paved the way for us to receive Their glory, to return to live with

Them, and to be perfected in body and in spirit. Now, with the plan laid out before us, all we need to do is live according to God's will. But what is God's will? It's the most valuable thing you can possess. There is nothing this world can offer that is more important than understanding the God who created the world. When you understand God, you can work to align your life with His will. And once you align your life with God's will, you can have eternal life and glory with Him through His Son, Jesus Christ.

The Apostle Paul said, "And if children, then heirs; heirs of God, and joint-heirs with Christ; if so be that we suffer with him, that we may be also glorified together" (Romans 8:17). This verse explains why alignment with God is the most valuable thing we can possess. If we suffer with Christ by taking His name upon us, we become a joint-heir with God and Christ. What is a joint-heir? Well, we know that a joint is where two objects come together and work as a single unit. In a body, it's where two different bones meet and work together as a single unit. The word *joint* is also used in banking, such as in "joint account." A joint account is an account owned by more than one person where each person on that account has full access to it. Each person can deposit and withdraw as much money as they like, whenever they want.

Now, what's an heir? We see the word *heir* used frequently regarding inheritances. Often the word is used when passing assets on to the next generation. Paul called us "heirs of God, and joint-heirs with Christ." What is Paul trying to tell us? He's saying that if we unite with God the Father and His Son, Jesus Christ, we become joint-heirs with God and Christ in their eternal glory. The most valuable and precious gift offered to us is the opportunity to be a joint-heir with Christ. So how do we obtain it?

Paul reveals how we can align ourselves with God and Christ so we can take advantage of all They offer: "Walk not after the flesh but after the Spirit" (Romans 8:1). That is the key to eternal glory with the Father and the Son. They have done Their part in creation, redemption, and in bringing us to perfection through Christ, but we must *choose* Christ to be perfected. God will never force us to follow Him. We must make a deliberate decision to follow Christ. Being a true Christian is not something you stumble upon. You cannot even be born a true Christian. Though you may be born into a Christian family, that does not make you a Christian.

True Christians have made a conscious decision to follow Christ through repentance and always striving to do His will. But how can we know the will of the Father and the Son? The answer to this question is also the answer to the question we asked at the outset of this chapter—how can we know that we must come to God through Jesus Christ? Through the Holy Ghost, or the Spirit. What exactly is the Holy Ghost? In Romans 8:1–16, Paul offers a sixteen-verse discourse on what the Spirit is and how the Spirit works. He then explains in Romans 8:17 the reward of living in the Spirit. In my own words according to Paul, being spiritually minded is to walk the strait-and-narrow path, which leads to our becoming an heir with God and joint-heir with Christ.

Now we can see the Godhead in its true light. God and Christ are members of the Godhead, perfected in body and spirit. The Holy Ghost is also a member of the Godhead but is different than God and Christ. He is different because the He is spirit only. But like God and Christ, the Holy Ghost knows the truth of all things; His knowledge and perfection are what bind Him to God and Jesus Christ. All three are perfectly unified in desire, motivation, will, and action—one in purpose. The Holy Ghost is responsible for leading and guiding us. Made up of spirit only, the Holy Ghost uses spiritual methods to communicate with us. Being that the Holy Ghost is spirit only, the concept of the Holy Ghost is difficult to understand and explain.

Similar to Jesus Christ, the Holy Ghost has many different names and descriptions that tell us who He is. These designations define the different roles of the Holy Ghost and our relationship with Him:

Spirit, Dove, Source of Testimony, Comforter, Holy Spirit, Gift of the Holy Ghost, Sign, Lord, Spirit of the Lord, Spirit of God, Spirit of Christ, Personage of Spirit, Witness, Cleanser, Purifier, Sanctifier, Testimony of Truth, Power of the Holy Ghost,

Companion, Baptism of Fire, Manifestation, Testimony of Christ, Conviction of Truth, Teach You All Things, Remembrance, Peace, Truth of All Things, Light, Protector, Inspiration of Truth, Quickeneth the Mind, Communicator, Pricked in the Heart, Prophecy, Bear Record, Spirit of Promise, Abide in Your Heart, Messenger, Revelator, Guide, Warmth, Spirit of Truth, and Still, Small Voice.

How can we explain something we cannot hear, see, smell, taste, or touch? The world cannot offer proof that the Holy Ghost exists. I personally can't prove it, and I'm not sure I can explain it. But I know I have felt His influence, and I know He is real. Let me explain. If we look back to the fighting example, we can see how the Holy Ghost plays a role similar to that of our corner. Let's analyze what a fighter experiences during a fight and see if there is anything similar to what happens to us in life.

Fighters often experience a burning in their lungs and shoulders due to the exhausting nature of a fight. Do we ever feel burned out and exhausted in life?

Getting hit in the face and head leads to the mind becoming confused, the body weak. In life, do we ever get hit with problems that make us feel confused and weak?

Getting hit in the body can cause a feeling of suffocation and restrict core movements. Have we ever taken a shot in life that makes us feel as if we can't go on? Have we ever felt that no matter how hard we try, we can't move beyond our current problems?

Cuts can lead to all kinds of distracting thoughts in a fight. Have you ever been cut from a team, job, friends, or family? I have been cut from all of the above, and I know that whenever I get hit with problems, all kinds of distracting thoughts start to creep into my mind. I lose track of my goals and start questioning my purpose, which often results in my taking the wrong direction due to my weak and troubled condition.

Fear of losing is the reason you are working so hard, but often fear leads only to anxiety and panic. And once anxiety and panic set in, fighters make bad decisions and lose fights. Have fear and panic ever made you work so hard you became counterproductive? I have experienced this in life, and I have experienced this in a fight. I have been filled with fear and panic that put me in a working frenzy. Although work is normally good, if you don't step back and look at the big picture and the goals you have in mind, all that work could be taking you in the wrong direction and become counterproductive to your original game plan.

Now let's look at your corner. In a fight, your corner's advice and encouragement is a strength and a comfort. Between rounds, you often feel like there is nothing more you can do. Your strength is gone, and you start to doubt your strategy. You wonder if you have the technique and ability necessary to beat your opponent. It is your corner's job to give you the confidence you need to go on, to remind you to give it all you have and stick to the game plan, or to change course depending on the situation. When the break between rounds is over and I'm done conversing with my corner, I get up off my stool and face my opponent with a greater confidence, knowing that as long as the fight is still on, I have a chance to win.

The strength and confidence that comes after consulting with my corner is similar to the feelings I have as I consult with the Holy Ghost. In a fight I can easily pinpoint the source of my newfound confidence. It comes when I get a quick break and some water between rounds and my corner and I have a chance to talk and evaluate the situation. It's all very hands-on—advice, rest, and water. All this leads to confidence, comfort, and more energy going into the next round. The break between rounds lifts my spirits and gives me a newfound motivation.

It's much the same in the fight of life. Even though it's not quite as hands-on, my spiritual Corner picks me up and keeps me moving when there seems to be no relief in sight. The Holy Ghost bolsters my confidence.

God has provided each of us with the opportunity to feel the Spirit. I'm sure you have felt the Holy Ghost even if you didn't define it as such. Take a look at the responsibilities of the Holy Ghost as found in John 14:26–27, and see if you can pinpoint the times you may have felt it.

> 26 But the *Comforter*, which is the Holy Ghost, whom the father will send in my name, he shall *teach* you all things, and

bring all things to your *remembrance* whatsoever I have said unto you.

27 *Peace* I leave with you, my peace I give unto you; *not as the world giveth*, give I unto you. Let not your heart be troubled, neither let it be afraid. (Emphasis added)

These two verses give us an idea of what the Holy Ghost can do for us. Let's look at the responsibilities of the Holy Ghost and the responsibilities of a corner side by side.

Life and the Holy Ghost	Fighting and Your Corner
Comforts	Comforts
In [Christ's] name	In the name of winning
Teaches	Teaches
Reminds	Reminds
Brings peace	Brings peace
Through spiritual means	Through physical means

Now that we understand a bit about the purpose of the Holy Ghost, let's look at times we may have felt His influence but did not recognize it as such. Most the time it does not come in a way we can easily recognize. The Holy Ghost's influence is an indescribable feeling brought to our spirit by a member of the Godhead. It often comes and goes with little to no recognition, but you have felt the Holy Ghost. If you don't think you have, you may be unaware of what His influence feels like. Or maybe you have felt the Holy Ghost and know you have, but you are in denial and don't want to admit you have felt something that confirms the reality of the Godhead. In this chapter we will cover why someone might try to avoid a personal testimony of the Godhead.

Have you ever learned new information regarding God or Christ and felt a peace and gained a deep personal conviction that the information was true? I have experienced these feelings many times throughout my life, starting as a child, such as when I was taught that God created all things. It simply made sense to me that there would be a Great Creator. There could never be any type of scientific information that could make me think otherwise. It's correct information regarding God that brings the confirmation of the Holy Ghost.

Even though I know God exists, I have considered the possibility that God may not actually exist. Whenever I've entertained this idea, I've felt empty and that my life had no purpose or reason. One key to recognizing the influence of Holy Ghost is learning to recognize when it is *not* present. I know the Holy Ghost is not present when I experience feelings of emptiness, fear, and doubt. I know when I consider the fact that there *is* a God, I feel confidence, peace, and love. When I think about the idea of there being a God versus the idea of there being no God, the latter limits my existence. If there is no God, it's game over when I die. I will no longer exist, and that feeling—knowing that death is the end of all things as I know it—fills me with anxiety, fear, and doubt. My personal relationships, along with my existence, could be over in an instant.

On the contrary, a belief in God's existence fills me with reassurance, which in turn gives me a sense of purpose. And when I think about the fact that the all-powerful Creator is a Creator with a purpose, I know God knows me and has a plan for me. My belief in a God who knows me and loves me is more than just excitement regarding the idea of God. It's a soul-quenching truth that leaves me feeling connected to Him, to Christ, and to the Holy Ghost, which connection allows me to experience spirit-to-spirit communication with Them.

God has provided a way for us to communicate with Him through the power of the Holy Ghost, but it is our responsibility to fine-tune our spiritual connection. Once you are able to recognize a prompting from the Holy Ghost, you'll have unlocked the most valuable treasure you can possess. What could be more important than a rewarding, intimate relationship with the three most powerful and loving beings in existence?

Some may say science is the reason people don't believe in God. But science is not disproving the theory that God exists; all science is doing is showing us the *ideas we previously had* concerning God may not be true. Misunderstanding God is not proof that God does not exist. And there is nothing wrong with not fully understanding God, because no one can ever truly fully understand God; once again, a full comprehension of God would make you a God. "Man doth not comprehend all things which the Lord can comprehend" (Mosiah 4:9) We do not have the capacity to fully understand God (see Jacob 4:8). Science may be able to shed new light on old religious concepts. A modern understanding may influence a current concept of God. But as far as *proof* that there is or is no God, there is none. And when there is no proof either way—you get to choose what you want to believe.

Many opt to believe there is no God, because no God means no consequences. Fear is the driving force behind atheism. Many people have been taught if they live a good life, they will go to heaven and if they live a bad life they will go to hell. Fear of hell causes people to question God's reality. They would rather no longer exist when they die than be punished by God or dwell in hell. People choose to believe there is no God because they fear they will not make the cut.

Today's mainstream belief systems leave us with three possible afterlife scenarios:

1. God is real, and I will receive His glory when I die.
2. God is real, but I will not be good enough to receive His glory, and I will be sentenced to hell when I die.
3. There is no God and therefore no existence after death.

I would like to dispel two of these beliefs and open your mind to the fact that there is actually only one option—eternal glory through Jesus Christ. How can glory through Christ be the only option? It's simple. The only requirement we need to obtain eternal glory is faith in Christ. We learn from the Pearl of Great Price, Abraham 3:22–26, that before we were born we had a full understanding of God, Christ, and Their plan for us. We exercised faith in Christ before we were born. Our faith came as we put our trust in Christ and acknowledged the fact that we believed Christ could create all things physical and overcome all things spiritual through the Atonement and Resurrection. The faith we exercised before we were born was the requirement to receive a body and obtain the opportunity to live on earth. Like it or not, every person who has ever lived on earth has already exercised faith in Christ. The faith we exercised in our premortal life qualified all of us to receive a body in this life, as well as a perfected body in the afterlife, through Christ's Resurrection.

Because of Christ's Atonement and Resurrection, we have the opportunity to be perfected not only in body but in spirit and to experience eternal joy despite the things we may have done wrong in this life. But we must acknowledge His sacrifice and repent. The Apostle Paul said, "Every knee shall bow to Jesus, and every tongue shall confess to God" (Romans 4:11). As we heed Paul's words, we allow the Atonement to cleanse our spirits, and our glory is made sure through Christ, God, and Their love for us.

God and Christ have done everything for you; by and through Them you will be lifted to eternal perfection. They are merciful beings, constant and true corners who want to see you win the fight and who are giving you expert advice to help you find success. But what happens if you chose not to listen to Them and follow Their counsel? Much as in the cage, if I lose a fight, I really only have myself to blame. It's not my corner's fault if I don't listen to him. And like I said, losing in MMA is the worst. When a fighter loses, it's a major hit to his ego, a punishment that hurts to his core and is filled with a sense of deep regret that he didn't do things differently.

In much the same way, we will receive our eternal punishment through our regret. That's right—regret equals hell. If you live your life and fail to acknowledge Their divinity, fail to heed Their counsel, you will regret it. Such regret will burn in your soul like fire. It will leave you gnashing your teeth and wishing you would have shown more love and devotion to God and Christ, knowing that God is the only being who could have brought you from nothing to a perfect, glorified state and that Christ suffered all things for you. Regret will come because you didn't give Them enough reverence or acknowledge Their hand in all things.

Knowing we will be saved because of our pre-existent faith, the fact that our knee will bow to Christ and our tongue will confess to God is a "treasure," or "pearl of great price" (Matthew 13:44–46). The test is what are we willing to do for Them. As we realize all that God and Christ have done for us, we become motivated by love for Them rather than by fear. As you let this realization sink into your soul, a desire to serve God will fill your heart because you love Them. The key is to know you are completely helpless without Them. Once you understand this, a love for God can grow in your heart.

Once your mind continually associates God with love—because you know everything you'll ever need is provided for you through God, Christ, and Their plan for you—you can now experience hope. We experience hope when we see our true potential. Before this realization, you may have been faced with belief options two and three, mentioned earlier:

> God is real, but I will not be good enough to receive His glory, and I will be sentenced to hell.
>
> God is not real, and there is no existence after death.

Hope is when even though we don't know if God exists we still want Him to. And we don't just want Him to exist, we also hope we can be glorified because of Him. Hope is exactly as it sounds. It's *hope*, or wishing for something. If you hope there is a God and that your glory is made sure through God and Christ, you have now planted a seed. If you let that seed of hope motivate you and then allow that motivation to turn into action, that action will be followed by gratitude. And a grateful heart leads to more action in serving God and Christ, whom you are not even sure exist. This service, which comes from an appreciation to a God you don't even know is real, is called faith. Faith is the requirement to know God.

Once you exercise faith through your actions, it's only a matter of time before God will reveal Himself to you through the power of the Holy Ghost. The way God reveals Himself unto you is up to God, Christ, and the Holy Ghost. Allow the Holy Ghost to be the Holy Ghost; don't try to tell God, Christ, or the Holy Ghost how to do Their job. They are Gods and know what They're doing.

To recap:

- Hope leads to appreciation.
- Appreciation leads to action.
- Action based on appreciation to God and Christ, who you don't have proof are real, equals faith.
- Faith is required to know God and Christ.
- Inconvenient actions of service based on hope alone constitute faith.
- Faith will result in God revealing Himself to you through the Holy Ghost.

Going out of your way to help and serve others because you want to serve a God you aren't even sure exists is the key to unlocking God's power and experiencing miracles. Patiently serving God is a demonstration of love you manifest to Him and those you serve. As you manifest love through your actions over a long period of time, you unlock the door, allowing God to reveal Himself to you through the Holy Ghost. Faith through action and appreciation consistently over time leads to our coming to know God and His Son and developing a connection with Them. But remember, it is on Their terms, not yours. The amount of faith required to know God is up to Them, not you.

But there is much you can do to express your faith. Now, I ask you to conduct an experiment in your mind and heart. Imagine that God *is* real and that you will receive His glory. Believe that as a fact for now. You now have hope. It's hope because you are not sure. It's just something you want to be true. If you want God to be real, you can now open your mind to His plan and disregard the fear of hell and the fear that motivates atheism.

Pay attention to the way you feel. You may be tempted to challenge the concept that all people will be perfected, saying that this means the wicked will receive the same reward as the righteous. We must keep in mind judgment and forgiveness are Christ's responsibility. You will never receive any lasting satisfaction condemning others to hell. It's not your job, and it will never make anything better. Regret for not following the Master is the only form of suffering we will truly experience. And we must not forget what Christ said concerning those who were mocking Him as they raised Him up on the cross: "Forgive them; for they know not what they do" (Luke 23:34). If we know Christ pled for mercy for the very people who crucified Him, how could we doubt that He loves all of God's children and is always willing forgive us?

And by the way, who crucified Him?

It's not easy to hear, but it was *you*. You crucified Him. I crucified Him. Everyone who has ever walked this earth and who will ever walk it played a part. And, ironically, each of us benefits from His suffering. The all-powerful Creator allowed Himself to be lifted up on the cross so we could be brought to perfection through Him. Christ suffered and endured all things for each one of us.

A Roman soldier may have driven the nails into His hands and feet, but it was your sins and my sins that required this unimaginable punishment to be laid upon the Lamb of God. A few men carried out the awful task of sacrificing the Lamb of God for the entire world as we know it, past, present, and future. But the man who pressed the sharp, cold steel against the hands of our Savior, raised his hammer, and hit the nail with a powerful and accurate blow represents the whole human family. In the court of Pilate, as Christ was sentenced to death, it was your voice raised against Him, crying, "Crucify him!" (Mark 15:13).

It is you and I who press the crown of thorns on His head and mock him when we put others down to build ourselves up (see Matthew 27:29). We are the ones who nail His hands and feet to the cross when we refuse to recognize His hand in all things. We lift the innocent Son of God up on the cross as we chase impure desires. And even as we torture Him in those moments of betrayal, he says to us, as well as to all who have lived an imperfect life, "Forgive them; for they know not what they do" (Luke 23:34).

One day you must stand before Christ at the Final Judgment. And if you haven't aligned yourself to God and Christ through the Holy Ghost, the anguish and regret you will experience at having played a part in torturing Him will be excruciating.

I can't stress enough how recognizing and acting on the promptings of the Holy Ghost is the most valuable thing you can do in life, because one day you will be brought before Christ and have a full recollection of everything you have done throughout your time on earth. At the same time, you will fully understand all that God and Christ have done for you. If you combine these two facts—fully knowing God and Christ and having a complete recollection of all your deeds, you will also see all that was happening for you spiritually. You will see that God and Christ continuously reached out to communicate with you throughout your life through the Holy Ghost, setting the stage for your eternal well-being. Recognizing the Holy Ghost and acting in accordance to His promptings is what will determine your peace of mind throughout eternity.

Whenever you feel confused, weak, like you can't go on, and that perfection and glory are unattainable, listen for the voice of your Corner, the Holy Ghost. He's there. He's got your back and your best interests at heart. And don't ever forget that He will be with you as you serve others. If you have ever wondered how the Holy Ghost works, serve! The peace you feel as you help others is the Holy Ghost letting you know your actions are recognized for good in God's eyes. Make it your lifelong goal to acquaint yourself with the Holy Ghost by tuning in to His voice amidst the deafening noise of life, through service to others, and by working hard to become the best fighter you can be.

Chapter 8
The Importance of Structure in Finding God

Some may think finding god is simple. It's not. You must get out of your comfort zone and structure your life in such a way that you can learn and progress. I've never seen a fighter who's content with his or her ability to fight; fighters always want to get better. It makes sense—you want to be as good as you can possibly be so you can win fights and avoid losing and getting hurt. Unfortunately, there are people who seem content with their relationship with God. Personally, seeking out and finding God has been one of my greatest joys.

One thing I often see when training fighters is that everyone thinks fighting is going to be easier than it is. Someone comes into the gym for the first time and expresses an interest in becoming a fighter. They sign up as a member of our gym and train in the fundamentals for a few weeks. When they are ready, they start sparring. Often, when they spar for the first time, they realize they are not very good at fighting and stop training. Quitting is a common trend I see among humans in all things. We get motivated. We set goals. We work toward those goals. We realize it's harder than we thought. We quit.

I bring this up not to motivate you to be a fighter but to motivate you to prioritize your goals. If finding God is your goal, stick with it.

We can't be good at everything, but we can strive to be better at something. Life presents us with many opportunities to grow and improve. But what things are worth your time? Family, school, career, and hobbies should be on our list of priorities, but continually seeking God should be our highest.

And why would we ever give up on finding God? I'll tell you why many people give up on finding God. It's the same reason people give up on pursuing any goal. It's harder than they think it will be. But finding God is much more important than getting good at fighting or passing a class at school. Finding God allows you to live in harmony with the most powerful being in existence. And living in harmony with Him will bring you clarity of mind and infuse you with power to overcome all the problems placed before you. Your problems may not be taken away, but your ability to handle those problems will increase if you are living in alignment with God. Then, as you look back on your life and see how God has given you the endurance to overcome trials, you will be blessed with an even stronger conviction that Jesus is your Savior, that God is your Father, and that the Holy Ghost is your guide.

As important as structure is to becoming a successful fighter, it's even more important for success in finding God. One thing you need to remember about life is that life is chaos; to have any success in the midst of chaos, you need a system that gives you direction.

With all the pressure and stress life throws at us, it's easy to feel weighed down. There's a strange human behavior in fighting that applies here. As fighters become fatigued, hurt, and beat up, they start making bad decisions. The stress and pressure of the fight becomes too much for them to handle. The mind starts looking for an easy way out, and fighters start making "home-run" moves—big punches and kicks that will end the fight as soon as they land. These big, fight-winning moves used at the wrong time often do more harm than good—for example, spinning side kicks, spinning back fists, or chasing submissions that aren't there and haven't been properly set up. I've been there, done that. We stray from the game plan when it gets hard.

Life is no different. Early in my fight career, I realized that the things I did to find the best way to fight were the same things I should be doing in life to find God. I call it "paralleling principles." In chapter 4 we talked about the four major arts of fighting—striking, wrestling, jiu-jitsu, ground and pound—and compared them to the fourfold mission of The Church of Jesus Christ of Latter-day Saints: perfect the Saints, proclaim the gospel, redeem the dead, and care for the poor and needy.

To these four core missions of the LDS Church, I would like to add a fifth—properly mixing these missions in your busy life. Mixing these missions so that none are neglected is a balancing act, for sure. Members of the LDS Church should strive to accomplish these missions in our lives on a monthly basis. We should work toward flawlessly mixing them by magnifying our callings, ministering to those around us, and looking for opportunities to talk about Christ. We should go to the temple at least once a month and participate in service activities as often as possible.

Properly balancing these missions provides members with lasting happiness that can only be earned through service. It is not a happiness brought to us based on personal achievement, nor is it happiness like that felt at a graduation, promotion, or upon receiving some type of award. Our goal is not to simply qualify for a heavenly promotion. Our goal is to help others because we love them.

If your main focus is love, you will find true happiness and fulfillment. And because all God does for us is based on love, you will tie yourself to Him because your desires are the same as His desires. As you love and serve others, you allow yourself to be motivated by what motivates God and Christ, and when you have the same desires as God and Christ, They will reveal Themselves to you through the Holy Ghost. The Holy Ghost will utilize Christ's Atonement, which will bring peace and lasting happiness to your soul. Love will have set in motion these moments of connection with Deity brought to you by the Holy Ghost.

When I look at the LDS Church, I see an organization set up to give its members structure and order. But structure and order to achieve what? Let's look at the fourfold mission again.

Perfect the Saints

The mission to perfect the Saints involves members of the Church looking out for members, just as a fighter looks out for the other members of his team. Within the Church are programs designed to help members become spiritually and physically healthy. All active adult members receive "callings" wherein they are asked to serve others with spiritual, emotional, and physical needs. Why are these callings important? The answer is simple: the stronger the body of the Church, the more effectively it can serve and help others. Healthy, strong members lead to a healthy, strong church. And a healthy, strong church is a church that can do great works in serving and helping others. What is the core motivation of work and service? It's *love*. The structure of the Church and the callings its members receive gives them a vehicle to express that love. Love should be your main building block while on your quest to find God. If you can develop a true love and appreciation for others, you can start to align yourself with God. A structured organization makes it easier to find opportunities to serve others. It matters not whether you are a member of the LDS Church, there are organizations you can join that will help you find ways to serve those in need.

Proclaim the Gospel

Why would we want to share the message of Jesus Christ with others? It's a lot like a coach sharing with fighters the things he knows will help them find success. We can all learn and benefit from the knowledge and experience of others. Much like the programs and training facilities available to help fighters learn and grow to become their best, the LDS Church also provides a structured approach to sharing powerful principles that lead to true happiness. For example, around the world are missionary training centers, where literally thousands upon thousands of missionaries go to learn the ropes so they can then go out into the world and share what they've learned. It is love for others and a desire for their success that motivates members to share.

Christ ties us to God through the Atonement. When you bind yourself to God through Christ, your life takes on meaning and purpose. You start to understand your eternal purpose when you see where you stand in relation to God, how much God loves you, and what He wants for you. You realize all that God has done for you and that even though you amount to nothing on your own, He still loves you. Your soul is, in turn, filled with love and gratitude and joy, and you naturally want others to feel this way. You long to share this message of love with others. That is what happens to true Christians who find God through Christ. It is a reflex. The first thing new Christians want to do is share the message of Christ so others can feel the peace, gratitude and joy they feel.

When we love our families, friends, and coworkers, we want them to understand that Christ can bring us to God through the Atonement. Love is the driving force for proclaiming the gospel. If love is the motivator for sharing the gospel, then let love also be your motivation for finding the gospel. If you are filled with love for others, you will find God because God *is* love. Do whatever it takes to fill your mind with love for others, even when it's not easy. Especially when it's not easy. My greatest challenge has been trying to love others when they are not helping me or may even be harming me. When we forgive and forget at all costs, we emulate Christ. When we push love out of our life, we begin to support the opposite of love, which is hate; and if God is love, Satan is hate. His power comes from the hate in our actions. The more we act on hate, the more hate fills others, and in this Satan gains power and authority over God's children.

God, Christ, and the Holy Ghost have eternal power over all things. God has allowed Satan to come to earth to tempt us to see how we will act when away from His physical presence. As we take on physical bodies that have natural tendencies that draw us away from God and toward Satan, Satan gains power. We ignore God when the desire for physical gratification becomes the priority, and anything that keeps us from our spiritual goals will foster the growth of hatred in our minds.

And when that hatred in our minds is manifested in our actions, Satan becomes more powerful. And that means there's more sadness and anger and discouragement in the world. Who needs more of that?

The good news is that God has already triumphed over Satan through the creation of the plan and the Atonement. God will triumph over Satan regardless of the amount of power Satan accumulates. When we emulate Christ with a forgiving heart, we allow love for others to fill our soul. When our love for others is more important than our personal agenda, we are following Christ's example. When our Christ-like actions fill our souls with happiness, these loving actions become a confirmation to us that God exists, that He loves us, and that we can connect to Him through love. And what could be better? Sharing what brings us happiness and ultimate success over our trials is a natural manifestation of our love for others.

Redeem the Dead

Just as there are certain standards a fighter must follow in order to be able to progress and participate, there are standards Christ has set for us to follow so that we might most effectively progress and participate in the building of His kingdom. One of these standards is baptism. Baptism is a physical symbol that we are willing to take Christ's name upon us. It could be compared to joining a training program and committing to follow the teachings of your trainer. No one can just walk in and expect to be trained without having gone through the proper channels.

Once you understand the importance of baptism for yourself, you will understand the need for *everyone* to be baptized, or to go through the proper channels. But how is baptism for all of God's children possible since billions have lived and died without knowing Christ?

As we briefly discussed in chapter 4, it's baptism for the dead—one of the ordinances that takes place in LDS temples. When people die—if they have accepted Christ and have been baptized in His name, with His authority, in His church, and have served Him faithfully—they become teachers in the spirit world. They understand Christ and His doctrine because they studied the scriptures and prayed as well as learned of Him through the Holy Ghost and through serving others. Because they learned of Christ and were willing to act on the knowledge they acquired, they became Saints, who, upon death, were ready to teach those who died but never knew or received Christ. The lost spirits who accept these teachings and Christ will have a chance to accept or reject the baptism performed for them by proxy in the temple.

Whether a soul has been baptized while on earth or in the next life does not matter (see Matthew 20:1–16; Luke 15). It does not matter when we come into Christ's kingdom. The hour we start working differs for each of us, depending on when we find the truth and decide to act upon it. Whether we accept our responsibility in this life or the next, the reward in Christ is set by Christ, and our reward in Christ will be given after our judgment, which will take place after the thousand-year period also known as the Millennium.

God created you as a spirit child in the premortal life. When it was your time to come to earth you passed through a veil and forgot your previous existence. Your spirit then united with your body sometime during gestation or at birth. Now, with your spirit and body united, you live on earth, and you will grow old and die. After death, your spirit will reside in a spirit world located here on earth, though it is like a fourth dimension we cannot see or detect. The spirit world is filled with those who have lived and died and who now are teaching or being taught God's plan. At some point in the future, Christ will return to the earth to reign as an all-powerful God.

This time is known as the Millennium. During the Millennium, covenant work such as baptism will continue to be done for the entire human family. Then, after the Millennium, there will be a final battle where Satan is allowed to make one last stand against Christ and His kingdom. After having been tested sufficiently as spirits, mortals, then spirits again, we will face one last challenge to see if we will stand for Christ in all thing as we fully comprehend the magnitude of our decision. We will face the temptations of Satan one last time, except this time we will have a complete understanding of God, Christ, and the Holy Ghost. God's plan will encompass the entire human family, every soul will be accounted for, and we all will be sufficiently prepared for our Final Judgment.

So what is the advantage of starting your employ in Christ's work now? We want to start working for Christ now because we receive happiness and authority as we work for Christ. God has power over all things in heaven and earth. God's power has been delegated to Jesus Christ, and you can receive a portion of that power by engaging in Their work. Our alignment with God and Jesus in Their kingdom brings eternal happiness. The joy I'm talking about can only be experienced by serving God and Christ and being filled with the Holy Ghost.

As I study God's plan of happiness, I feel deep gratitude that we have the opportunity to work for God. I know as I exercise faith and accept my responsibility to Christ, I can look forward to the day when I can kneel before my Savior and confess that He is the Christ. Understanding the plan does not bring me fear. It brings gratitude and an excitement to serve, and that is why we want to start working for Christ as soon as we can. It's not because we have to but because we can't wait to serve our Creator. Once the desire to serve Christ possesses your soul, you know you have found the same God found by Adam, Noah, Abraham, Isaac, Jacob, Joseph, Moses, David, Elijah, Isaiah, Jeremiah, Daniel, the Twelve Apostles of Christ, and Paul. I did not mention all the prophets, but I hope you get the point. These men dedicated their lives to the Lord not out of fear but because of the gratitude they had toward God. Their gratitude toward God transformed in their hearts to love for others. And it's love for others that motivates the work of redeeming the dead.

Care for the Poor and Needy

I started doing service projects when I was about twelve years old. I wish I could say I did them because I personally wanted to, but I didn't.

I did them because I had to. That's right—I was expected to. As a young man in an LDS family, I was expected to go to activities every Tuesday evening at seven. Sometimes these activities were organized by the Church, other times by the local Boy Scout program. Either way, my parents insisted I participate. It was simple logic for them. They'd provided me with shelter, food, and clothes and, in return, they expected me to participate in service activities. To keep the peace, I went along with it. But often these activities were just a long, boring feat of endurance. I still remember looking at my watch and counting the minutes until I could go home. The bottom line is that my heart wasn't in it. I didn't do it because I wanted to and because I loved the people but because I was expected to.

Does that mean it was a waste of time? I don't think so. It was strange, but whenever I was done serving, it felt good knowing I'd helped someone in need. So even though it wasn't my idea of a good time and I often didn't want to be there, it was time well spent. If you think about the other ways I could have spent my time as a teenager, not only were service projects good, they probably kept me out of trouble.

My service as a teenager represented the love and compassion my church leaders had for others. These leaders were kind, caring adults who were concerned with me and the people we served. They were aware of the needs in our neighborhood and in the local area. I even remember sewing quilts for families around the world.

These wise adult leaders saw a need and were able to gather the youth to help out. It was being involved in these projects that strengthened my testimony of service. It defies logic that even though I complained about the service we were providing and didn't want to be there, I always felt a sense of love and peace in the end.

Why do we care for the poor and needy? I would hope it's because we love the people we are serving, but even if we don't, we should help anyway. Simply getting out and serving others is one of the ways we exercise faith, as talked about in the Book of Mormon in Alma 32. It's like planting a seed. What happens as we serve when we have to is that our love and appreciation for those we serve grows. As we serve, we feel more love. That love leads us to serve God's children more, and we begin to feel aligned with God, who does all things for His children.

You'll find that by planting that seed and aligning yourself with Him in love for His children by serving them, your testimony will grow so that it cannot be shaken by anything people say to convince you otherwise. When your testimony is grounded in God through service and love, it becomes a sure knowledge of God's goodness.

Try it. Plant a seed of faith, go out and serve someone, you'll feel a greater connection with God. If it does not work, at least you helped someone in need. If it does, you have created a win-win—you've helped others and developed a connection with God.

Let's take a closer look at Alma's discussion on planting a seed of faith. I will quote Alma 32:26–43 here and then again. The second time, I will change a few words around:

> 26 Now, as I said concerning faith—that it was not a perfect knowledge—even so it is with my words. Ye cannot know of their surety at first, unto perfection, any more than faith is a perfect knowledge.
>
> 27 But behold, if ye will awake and arouse your faculties, even to an experiment upon my words, and exercise a particle of faith, yea, even if ye can no more than desire to believe, let this desire work in you, even until ye believe in a manner that ye can give place for a portion of my words.
>
> 28 Now, we will compare the word unto a seed. Now, if ye give place, that a seed may be planted in your heart, behold, if it be a true seed, or a good seed, if ye do not cast it out by your unbelief, that ye will resist the Spirit of the Lord, behold, it will begin to swell within your breasts; and when you feel these swelling motions, ye will begin to say within yourselves—It must needs be that this is a good seed, or that the word is good,

for it beginneth to enlarge my soul; yea, it beginneth to enlighten my understanding, yea, it beginneth to be delicious to me.

29 Now behold, would not this increase your faith? I say unto you, yea; nevertheless it hath not grown up to a perfect knowledge.

30 But behold, as the seed swelleth, and sprouteth, and beginneth to grow, then you must needs say that the seed is good; for behold it swelleth, and sprouteth, and beginneth to grow. And now, behold, will not this strengthen your faith? Yea, it will strengthen your faith: for ye will say I know that this is a good seed; for behold it sprouteth and beginneth to grow.

31 And now, behold, are ye sure that this is a good seed? I say unto you, yea; for every seed bringeth forth unto its own likeness.

32 Therefore, if a seed groweth it is good, but if it groweth not, behold it is not good, therefore it is cast away.

33 And now, behold, because ye have tried the experiment, and planted the seed, and it swelleth and sprouteth, and beginneth to grow, ye must needs know that the seed is good.

34 And now, behold, is your knowledge perfect? Yea, your knowledge is perfect in that thing, and your faith is dormant; and this because you know, for ye know that the word hath swelled your souls, and ye also know that it hath sprouted up, that your understanding doth begin to be enlightened, and your mind doth begin to expand.

35 Oh then, is not this real? I say unto you, yea, because it is light; and whatsoever is light, is good, because it is discernible, therefore ye must know that it is good; and now behold, after ye have tasted this light is your knowledge perfect?

36 Behold I say unto you, nay; neither must ye lay aside your faith, for ye have only exercised your faith to plant the seed that ye might try the experiment to know if the seed was good.

37 And behold, as the tree beginneth to grow, ye will say: let us nourish it with great care, that it may get root, that it may grow up, and bring forth fruit unto us. And now behold, if ye nourish it with much care it will get root, and grow up, and bring forth fruit.

38 But if ye neglect the tree, and take no thought for its nourishment, behold it will not get any root; and when the heat of the sun cometh and scorcheth it, because it hath no root it withers away, and ye pluck it up and cast it out.

39 Now, this is not because the seed was not good, neither is it because the fruit thereof would not be desirable; but it is because your ground is barren, and ye will not nourish the tree, therefore ye cannot have the fruit thereof.

40 And thus, if ye will not nourish the word, looking forward with an eye of faith to the fruit thereof, ye can never pluck of the fruit of the tree of life.

41 But if ye will nourish the word, yea, nourish the tree as it beginneth to grow, by your faith with great diligence, and patience, looking forward to the fruit thereof, it shall take root; and behold it shall be a tree springing up unto everlasting life.

42 And because of your diligence and your faith and your patience with the word in nourishing it, that it may take root in you, behold, by and by ye shall pluck the fruit thereof, which is most precious, which is sweet above all that is sweet, and which is white above all that is white, yea, and pure above all that is pure; and ye shall feast upon this fruit even until ye are filled, that ye hunger not, neither shall ye thirst.

43 Then, my brethren, ye shall reap the rewards of your faith, and your diligence, and patience, and longsuffering, waiting for the tree to bring forth fruit unto you.

As you experiment on these words, it's important you do so with a true understanding of what faith is. James chapter 2 tells us over and over that faith and works are one and the same. Let's see what happens when we replace each instance of the word *faith* with some form of *love and service* in the verses in Alma. I will also adapt or expound on the text so that it makes more sense in this context and so you'll have a good idea of how exercising faith, or love and service, brings us great joy and peace:

> 26 Now, as I said concerning *love and service—you do not do it because you know God—because you cannot know God with my words*. Ye cannot know of their surety at first, unto perfection, *because action is what is required in order to obtain* a perfect knowledge.
>
> 27 But behold, if ye will awake and arouse your faculties, even to an experiment upon my words, and exercise a particle of *love and service*, yea, even if ye can no more than desire to *love and serve*, let this desire work in you, even until ye believe in a manner that ye can give place for a portion of my words.
>
> 28 Now, we will compare *love and service* unto a seed. Now, if ye give place, that a seed of *love and service* may be planted in your heart, behold, if it be a true seed, or a good seed, if ye do not cast it out by your unbelief, that ye will resist the Spirit of the Lord, behold, it will begin to swell within your breasts; and when you feel these swelling motions, ye will begin to say within yourselves—It must needs be that this is a good seed, or that *love and service* is good, for it beginneth to enlarge my soul; yea, it beginneth to enlighten my understanding, yea, it beginneth to be delicious to me.
>
> 29 Now behold, would not this increase your faith *and feelings of love for others? Which is works in a good cause such as caring for the poor and the needy*. I say unto you, yea; nevertheless, it hath not grown up to a perfect knowledge [*because you do not have physical proof of God*].
>
> 30 But behold, *as your works in love and service* swelleth, and sprouteth, and beginneth to grow, then you must needs say that the seed is good; for behold it swelleth, and sprouteth, and

beginneth to grow. And now, behold, will not this strengthen your *desire to love and serve others?* Yea, it will strengthen your *desire to love and serve others: because good works promote good works.* For ye will say I know that this is a good seed; for behold it sprouteth and beginneth to grow.

31 And now, behold, are ye sure that this is a good seed? I say unto you, yea; for every seed bringeth forth unto its own likeness.

32 Therefore, if a seed groweth it is good, but if it groweth not, behold it is not good, therefore it is cast away.

33 And now, behold, because ye have tried the experiment, and planted the seed *of caring for the poor and the needy*, and it swelleth and sprouteth, and beginneth to grow, ye must needs know that the seed is good.

34 And now, behold, is your knowledge perfect? Yea, your knowledge is perfect in that thing, and your faith is dormant [*meaning faith as a desire, because the desire has turned to action, and action has brought knowledge*]; and this because you know, for ye know that the word hath swelled your souls, and ye also know that it hath sprouted up, that your understanding doth begin to be enlightened, and your mind doth begin to expand.

35 Oh then, is not this real? I say unto you, yea, because it is light; and whatsoever is light, is good, because it is discernible [*meaning you can sense the reality of God*], therefore ye must know that it is good; and now behold, after ye have tasted this light is your knowledge perfect?

36 Behold I say unto you, nay; neither must ye lay aside your works, *because if you do not nourish your good works and continue in love and service, you will forget the light and peace that was brought to your soul, and your sure knowledge of God can be lost because you neglected to nourish the seed of love and service,* for ye have only exercised your *love* to plant the seed that ye might try the experiment to know if the seed was good.

37 And behold, as the tree beginneth to grow, ye will say: let us nourish it with great care, that it may get root, that it may grow up, and bring forth fruit unto us. And now behold, if ye nourish it with much care it will get root, and grow up, and bring forth fruit. [*If you continue in love and service over a long period of time, your knowledge of God will take root in your soul. Finding God through actions of love promotes further loving actions, and your life of service is the fruit of finding God.*]

38 But if ye neglect the tree, and take no thought for its nourishment, behold it will not get any root; and when the heat of the sun cometh and scorcheth it, because it hath no root it withers away, and ye pluck it up and cast it out. [*If you don't continue in love and service over a long period of time, when hard times come, your belief in God and in good works will be lost.*]

39 Now, this is not because *love and service* are not good, neither is it because the fruit thereof would not be desirable; but it is because your ground is barren, and ye will not nourish the tree, therefore ye cannot have the fruit thereof.

40 And thus, if ye will not care for the poor and the needy, looking forward with an eye of *love and service* to the fruit thereof, ye can never pluck of the fruit of the tree of life.

41 But if ye will nourish the word, yea, nourish the tree as it beginneth to grow, by your *actions of love* with great diligence, and patience, looking forward to the fruit thereof, it shall take root; and behold it shall be a tree springing up unto everlasting life.

42 And because of your diligence and *your love for others* and your patience . . . in nourishing it, that it may take root in you, behold, by and by ye shall pluck the fruit thereof, which is most precious, which is sweet above all that is sweet, and which is white above all that is white, yea, and pure above all that is pure; and ye shall feast upon this fruit even until ye are filled, that ye hunger not, neither shall ye thirst.

43 Then, my brethren, ye shall reap the rewards *as you care for others*, and your diligence, and patience, and long-suffering, waiting for the tree to bring forth fruit unto you.

When I read Alma 32 this way, it helps me see how important it is to act. The reward of a life dedicated to serving others because you want to know God is that you gain a love for others. And as you love and serve others, you serve God. Because you serve God, you will know God. You will be aligned with God in desire and actions. These desires and actions are the same as those held by Christ and the Holy Ghost, and you will come to know Them as well.

Christ spent his whole life caring for the poor and needy. As you read the scriptures and see the word *faith*, change that word to *love*, *serve*, and *care for the poor and needy*. You'll see that acting in *faith* is synonymous to acting in love for others:

Luke 22:32

> But I have prayed for thee, that thy faith fail not: and when thou art converted, strengthen thy brethren.
>
> But I have prayed for thee, that thy [love and service] fail not: and when thou art converted, strengthen thy brethren.

Acts 15:9

> And put no difference between us and them, purifying their hearts by faith.
>
> And put no difference between us and them, purifying their hearts by [loving and serving].

2 Corinthians 4:13

> We having the same spirit of faith, according as it is written, I believed, and therefore have I spoken; we also believe, and therefore speak.
>
> We having the same spirit of [love and service], according as it is written, I believed, and therefore have I spoken; we also believe, and therefore speak.

This exchange works on so many levels. I don't want to add or take away from the words of the prophets and apostles, but what this has shown me is that, truly, faith without works is dead (see James 2:17). *Faith* is an action word.

At one time I thought faith was just a belief, desire, or hope. But belief, desire, and hope are what precede faith. They are the building blocks. If you profess to believe in Christ, you desire to act as Christ acts and you hope He will redeem you from your sins. This desire will take root in you and change your character. And though we know we cannot earn our way to Christ through actions, we are compelled to act as Christ because we love Christ and others.

So, again, why do we care for the poor and needy? It may start out because we are expected to, or it may be because we just want to discover God through service. Whatever the reason, I hope your motivation for serving others eventually turns into pure love for them and for Christ.

Just as with all the other missions of the LDS Church, it's the doing with love that counts. If we want to truly grow and develop a meaningful connection to God and with His children, we must be motivated by love. If your motivation for serving others is not pure love, don't give up. Continue to serve until that effort brings love to your heart. Eventually your motivation will truly change, and you will be driven by love.

Chapter 9

Fighting with Your Eternal Family and Fighting for Your Eternal Family

CERTAINLY MY FIRST FIGHTS WERE with my family. I remember as a very young child punching and kicking my brothers and sister over silly things like toys. According to the Merriam-Webster dictionary one way to define fighting is "to struggle, to endure, or surmount." Recognizing we all struggle against our families at one time or another opens my mind to the fact that much of our struggle in life is with our loved ones. I have fought many real, physical fights in my life. In a real MMA fight, it's comforting to know the fight will only last fifteen minutes, depending on the type of fight. If we contrast that with the struggles we face with our families, it makes a simple fifteen-minute fight look silly and meaningless. I'm sure the struggle with my loved ones will be the longest, hardest battle I will ever fight.

Why do we fight with our families? I think the reason we fight so often with loved ones is because we are basically selfish beings who think we always know what's right. In wanting what's best for our families, it's easy to believe we know what they need. At the same time, they think they know what's best for us.

It begins with young parents trying to rear their children in the most appropriate way possible, teaching them discipline, obedience, and self-restraint. But kids who are full of energy and spunk are a recipe for conflict. I've seen it everywhere—at the store, at public events, at the gym, at church—you name it; young kids can be a ticking time bomb. Soon these kids grow to be teenagers, their energy is still high, and we still have a recipe for conflict, but the conflict becomes more serious and usually happens behind slammed doors. Then teenagers become adults who need to make their own life decisions, and often young adults and their parents do not see eye to eye.

In addition to the struggles between parents and children, there are fights between siblings and even between extended family members. But probably the most sinister fighting within the family is between husbands and wives. Fights between spouses are the most serious because they can lead to divorce and the breakup of the family.

Interestingly, most all family disputes stem from a mixture of love and selfishness. The challenge is figuring out which we are motivated by. I hope that in understanding why we are fighting we can cut down on the amount of fighting within the family. The key is to cut down on selfish behavior and add more love. Selfish behavior promotes fighting within the family, and oftentimes fighting within the family results in families deciding to spend less time together.

Love connects the family; selfish behavior breaks it up. Love connects you with God; selfish behavior separates you from Him. I truly believe love is what connects us to our families and to God because, as our Father, God is family also. As love for God grows, love for our family will also grow.

When you find that love is how you connect to God, it's natural to be drawn to your family. I understand that in some cases the family is the cause of much heartache and sorrow, but if you look at the family in its purest form, we can see the need for parents. We need parents to obtain our physical bodies. Once we are born, we need parents or guardians to take care of us. We cannot live on our own, so it takes the loving heart of a guardian to keep us alive. The love of our parents creates the foundation of love in our lives. If they have loved and cared for us, it's natural for us to then love and care for our own children.

For me, loving others has been somewhat difficult at times as many of the people in my life have challenged my goals and plans. But with both my son and daughter, it's different. I don't seem to mind the challenges they bring to my life. As parents, our children often create problems for us, but because we love them, we are willing to deal with the inconvenience.

In our early years, we need parents and guardians; in our old age, we often need the support of our children to keep us comfortable in our final years. A healthy, loving family is the foundation for building love in our lives.

Those of you blessed—yes, blessed—with a dysfunctional family have an opportunity to make something from nothing. Creating something with your hands that takes time, discipline, and hard work brings a great deal of satisfaction, especially when it's created from nothing. When you come from a dysfunctional family and create a functional family, it's the same. If you were brought up in an abusive or a neglectful family situation, you can break the cycle and create a loving, nurturing family of your own. I know people who came from broken families who, despite the bad examples in their lives, rose to the challenge and created functional, loving families for themselves. Oftentimes people don't appreciate what they have unless they have experienced worse. It is because of this contrast that we are able to experience joy.

Family life is the foundation for connecting with God. In Malachi 4:5–6, we read the prophecy of Elijah: "And he shall turn the hearts of the fathers to the children, and the hearts of the children to their fathers, lest I come and smite the earth with a curse." These are the last words in the Old Testament. It's as if they were put there to prepare our minds to find Christ in the New Testament, but they also prepare us to receive Christ when we finally meet Him, whether at our judgment or at His Second Coming.

Why do I say Malachi 4:6 prepares us to find Christ? Family is where we develop our capacity to love, and the essence of Christ is love. If you are a loving person and are concerned with the welfare of others, the message of Christ will resonate with your soul. You can see it in two different ways. If you have been developing love through strong family ties, you are prepared to have the message of Christ resonate in your soul. If you don't have a strong family, and the message of Christ rings true to you, your desire will be to create a family and bring love into your own household. You will share with your children the teachings of Christ. Christ will draw you to your family, and the love of your family will draw you to Christ.

If you have filled your thoughts and life with love, you will have a desire to connect with your family. The desire to connect to your family is the byproduct of being a loving person. When you turn to God through love, your heart naturally turns to your parents, grandparents, and ancestors. Your heart will also turn toward your children and grandchildren and beyond.

When love motivates you to find God, that love will fill your heart, and you will be motivated to turn toward your family. This is a sign you have found the same God as Abraham, Isaac, and Jacob. Throughout the Bible we find the lineages that tie us to Adam, which shows us our divine potential, because God created Adam in His image.

Adam descended from God, and we descended from Adam, which is a testament of our divine lineage. We are all God's creations, created in His image. But what happens to our brothers and sisters who never receive Christ in their lives? As mentioned in our discussion of the fourfold mission of the LDS Church, we can redeem our brothers and sisters from past generations in the Lord's temples.

We previously talked about how every knee shall bow and every tongue shall confess that Jesus is the Christ and how the grace and Atonement of Christ qualify us to receive a perfected body and spirit. So what is the advantage of exercising faith in Christ before our final judgment? Let me change some words around to see if I can shed new light on the importance of faith:

"You can exercise faith in Christ by following His example."

"You can exercise *responsibility* in Christ by following His example."

Why would I change the word *faith* to *responsibility*? Because being a Christian is a responsibility. Once Christ has made Himself known unto you through the power of the Holy Ghost, it is your responsibility to act like a Christian. Often we don't receive Christ's truth because we don't have the courage to act on it. It's likely that, more often than not, we are not ready to receive certain revelations, even when we think we are. Those who are willing to be responsible and act as Christians are witnesses to some of the greatest miracles. If you have not witnessed miracles, change the way you think. Be willing to serve Christ in all things. Once you are honest in heart and willing to sacrifice your desires for Christ, you are ready to experience miracles.

Baptism is a perfect example of taking on responsibility as a Christian. Baptism constitutes a promise between you and God symbolized by an action. The promise is that you will always remember Christ and keep His commandments. The action is following His example and demonstrating faith by being baptized in His name. As you keep that promise and continue to follow Christ's example by living a Christ-centered life, you will receive responsibilities in Christ's name.

Our level of responsibility is what sets the stage for our final state with Christ after our judgment. We will all receive grace and be resurrected, but our final state of existence with Christ is determined by the responsibility we take on as we learn of Christ throughout our premortal, mortal, and postmortal existence.

How did we demonstrate faith in Christ before we were born? How did we demonstrate our allegiance to Christ by fulfilling our responsibilities for Christ in the premortal life? In the premortal life, we dwelt with God and Christ in a spiritual existence. The Father presented a plan whereby we could progress and return to Him in a perfect physical and spiritual existence. In Christ plan we would be given a body and be tested through temptation, sin, and pain so that we could exercise our agency and gain knowledge and experience. We knew it wouldn't be easy, but our acceptance of Christ's plan in our premortal state is what constituted our pre-earth faith in Christ. We knew Christ would do His part to carry out the plan and bring us back to God if we repented and accepted His Atonement.

At the same time, we were presented with another plan, Satan's plan, wherein he would be our savior and save us from pain. Satan could have saved us from pain if we would have chosen his plan and not come to earth. No earth life, no body, and therefore, no pain. It sounds like a good deal but Satan's plan would void our progression and take away our ability to make our own choices and experience the joys of life. Thus, we would be subject to Satan and be damned for eternity. Satan wanted to save us from pain by never introducing us to pain. Satan's campaign to save us from pain is still alive today in the form of illegal drugs, alcohol, and suicide which are used to help us avoid pain. Satan has always offered the easy way out. The fact is pain and problems are part of Christ's plan. As we struggle through and overcome life's trials we accept Christ and His plan.

Our premortal faith came as we aligned ourselves with the Father and chose Christ's plan. The fact that we are alive today is evidence that we chose His plan. Everyone who has ever lived exercised faith in Christ before they were born.

What responsibilities do we have in Christ's kingdom while here on earth? How do we demonstrate our allegiance to Christ by fulfilling our responsibilities to Him in this life?

In His infinite wisdom, God has blessed us with the unique opportunity to be sealed to our family in the Lord's temples. Being sealed to our family means our relationship with them will endure throughout eternity. Not only do we bind our families together by allowing our deceased ancestors to be baptized, we can also have our families *sealed* to us forever. When members of the LDS Church refer to "temple work," they are talking about performing ordinances that allow all people to be bound to God and to their families for eternity. One example of an ordinance that allows families to be sealed is temple marriage. When members of the LDS Church are married in the temple, it is for time and all eternity, which is different from a regular marriage, which is when people vow to love and support one another "until death do us part."

But being sealed to your family is not a given, and it's not easy. Many of us cannot maintain strong family relationships in this life, let alone throughout eternity. One key to being sealed to your family for eternity is to "seal" yourself to your family now. I mean spend time with them. If there is a problem tearing your family apart, fix it *now*. Take a look at what you can do to repair any damage you may have caused. This is your responsibility in this life. Whatever the issue may be, get over it. Humble yourself and admit you were wrong. As you do your best to overcome family issues now, you prepare yourself to find love through family and Christ. Because it is key to our happiness and to finding God, we must all fight for our eternal family and take advantage of the temple work The Church of Jesus Christ of Latter-day Saints offers.

Chapter 10
Your Greatest Weapon

Throughout this book we've looked at how fighting and finding God are similar. One of the greatest factors in my personal quest to know God is the Book of Mormon. As my moral compass, the Book of Mormon has changed my life for the better and solidified my belief in God. It is through the teachings of this book that I've found my greatest happiness and success in all aspects of life that truly matter.

My Story

It all started in ninth grade when I was fourteen years old. I was in an LDS seminary class and was given the challenge to read the Book of Mormon by the end the school year. Considering I was a very slow reader, that was a daunting task. The Book of Mormon is 531 pages long. All throughout school I was in either resource or special-ed classes, and I continually fell behind in every class. School and reading were not my thing, but I took on the challenge anyway and committed to read a chapter a day and finished the Book of Mormon when I was fifteen.

I'll be honest: I understood nothing I read, but I did feel peace and was glad I read it. But those teen years can be crazy. From ages fifteen to eighteen, I was active in the LDS Church and fulfilled my church callings and responsibilities, but outside of church, when I was with my friends, I was a bit wild and ran with a rough crowd. Let's just say we knew how to find trouble and have fun. My priorities as a teenager were first, sports (wrestling and then football); second, friends; and third, church. That's right—I left school off the list. I hated school.

I only went to school so I could wrestle and play football. I should not have graduated from high school, but I was good friends with the principal, who was a big fan of wrestling. Often he would come to practice and work out with me. He made a deal with me. If I would do a few simple things, he would make sure my teachers gave me a passing grade so I could graduate.

This set the stage for the worst deal I ever made. As captain of the football and wrestling teams, I was extremely athletic. In a high school weight-lifting tournament where we competed against all the other high schools in Utah, I won first place and set a new high school weight-lifting record. That made me extremely valuable as a football player. In wrestling, I took second in state as a junior and first in state as a senior. Earning these awards led me to believe I would get a college scholarship and continue to compete as a college athlete.

As an arrogant high school senior, I made a deal with the Lord. I told Him I would serve a full-time mission if I didn't get an athletic scholarship to play sports in college. Well, that had to be a good deal for God. Early in the football season, I broke my hand and was off the field when the recruiters came through. Then, I won state in wrestling and went to a national wrestling tournament in Delaware where all the college recruiters went to scout out new talent for college wrestling teams. All I had to do was place to get a scholarship. I won my first match but separated my rib in my second, which I lost. I went on and wrestled the third match with a separated rib. In the third round of that third match, the same rib got smashed, and I lost that match as well. It was that easy—a few injuries and my chances for a college scholarship were gone.

Now I had a problem: I'd said I would go on a mission if I did not get a college scholarship. The problem was I was not sure I believed the Book of Mormon. Even though I'd read it at age fifteen and liked it, I just was not sure I believed it enough to justify leaving on a two-year mission and teaching other people about it. At age eighteen I figured I needed to read it again, so I started with a chapter a day. I understood the Book of Mormon a little better the second time around, but even then my comprehension was very limited.

It didn't take long till I came across this verse in 2 Nephi 4:34:

> O Lord, I have trusted in thee and I will trust in thee forever. I will not put my trust in the arm of the flesh; for I know that cursed is he that putteth his trust in the arm of the flesh. Yea, cursed is he that putteth his trust in man or maketh flesh his arm.

The message hit me full force. I knew at that moment that I had to serve a full-time two-year LDS mission. As I have reflected on that scripture, I have tried to figure out why it had such a powerful effect on me. Earlier that year I had suffered two major injuries. One day I felt I was the best football player around; the next day, due to my injuries, I could not pick up a can of soda. One day I felt I could throw anyone I wanted right to their back; the next, I could not even get out of a chair without help. My whole life I thought I was strong, but I soon came to realize that I was only a man and that I was weak.

Let me explain what I felt as I read 2 Nephi 4:34. When Joseph Smith read James 1:5, he said, "Never did any passage of scripture come with more power to the heart of man than this did at this time to mine. It seemed to enter with great force into every feeling of my heart" (Joseph Smith—History 1:12). When I read 2 Nephi 4:34, I likewise had never before felt anything so powerful. From that moment on, I could not wait to serve a mission. Not only did I want to give God two years of my life, I wanted to give God my whole life. If I could have somehow given my entire life to God forever, I would have done it.

That feeling was so powerful and so good I would have done anything to keep it with me. In that moment, I knew God existed. And not only did I know there was a God and that God created the universe, I knew that He knew my name. *He knew my name!* And I knew He loved me. I knew He had a work for me to do. I felt a power, but it was not my power; it was God's. In that moment, I knew I was weak, but an impression came to my mind. If I aligned my will with God's, I could use His power to do His work. I could be a tool in His hands and bring forth His glory on His earth. That was an amazing feeling.

After reading 2 Nephi 4:34 that night, I was on fire. I told anyone who would listen about the gospel. I remember talking to my LDS friends and telling them they needed to read the Book of Mormon and go on a mission. I told my non-LDS friends they had to read the Book of Mormon and that it would change their lives for the better.

I finished the Book of Mormon at the age of nineteen, before I went on my mission to the Washington DC South Mission. I continued to read the Book of Mormon every day onward and even after my mission. I'm not sure how many times I have read the Book of Mormon now, but I know I constantly discover new things and receive greater motivation to serve Christ every time I read it. I would like to share a few things I could only learn from the Book of Mormon.

Early in my mission, I was reading the introduction to the Book of Mormon and came across the sixth paragraph where Joseph Smith declared, "I told the brethren that the Book of Mormon was the most correct of any book on earth, and the keystone of our religion, and a man would get nearer to God by abiding by its precepts than by any other book." What a bold statement. Could Joseph Smith really say that about the Book of Mormon? I thought about it for days. I kept thinking about it being the "most correct book on earth" and that "a man would get nearer to God by abiding by its precepts than by any other book." I felt like I was being challenged to find that error in the book and to see if it was getting me as close to God as Joseph Smith said it would.

I admit investigating the Book of Mormon on my mission may have created some preconceived notions and biased opinions, but on the other hand, what a great time to study its truths and test its promises, for two reasons. First, I was required to study scripture for two hours a day. At what other time in my life would I have two hours a day to study scriptures? Second, as I talked to people about the Book of

Mormon every day, I heard everything you could imagine about it. In the Washington DC South area, there were many Christians and educated people. I was always talking to people who were familiar with the Book of Mormon, whether from a history or religion class they took or from learning about the Book of Mormon at church or from friends and relatives. Many churches actually taught their members how to talk to Mormons. That gave me a great chance to learn how people felt about it. Not always, but often, people had heard unpleasant things about Mormons and the Book of Mormon and despised the book.

As I have had religious conversations with people, I find there is often an intellectual pecking order among those who have considered godly questions.

Let's talk about that pecking order. First, atheists and agnostics come across as very smart, logical people, believing only that which they can prove through unbiased science. Next, there are those who will give you the typical arguments on how they can *prove* God's existence, but it's never proof. It may be evidence, but it's not proof. If the believer's arguments held up under scientific law, we would be teaching "God's universal law" in schools and universities. We don't teach it because we can't prove it. I think God made it that way. Believers are not dumb people. What they lack in proof, they make up for in faith. We've all heard it: "You must have faith." The debate goes on and on. Lastly, you will find people who are a part of a major belief system, such as Christians, Muslims, Jews, Buddhists, and Hindus. When one believer in God debates another believer in God, it now comes down to doctrine, godly logic, or just trying to prove historical facts that support one's beliefs.

Many people throughout my mission made it a point to prove me wrong about the Book of Mormon using a common tactic. No matter their background, I could hear them thinking, *Eric, you must be dumber than I thought you were. How can you believe that book?* And I'm not talking about strangers I met on my mission, though that was often the case. Many of the people who've attacked my intelligence are people I have had close relationships with.

I have studied both sides of the argument; my final conclusion being that you cannot *prove* the Book of Mormon right or wrong! As I said about trying to prove whether God is real, I believe God made it that way. Part of the plan is to leave us to our devices to see what we will do in a world with no real proof of why we are here or where we came from.

I couldn't and still can't prove the Book of Mormon is true or that God exists, but does the Book of Mormon bring me nearer to God by abiding by its precepts?

Throughout my fighting career, I've been fortunate to have mentors and corners who have guided me through the toughest fights and helped me see some of my greatest successes. It's been the same in my fight to find God. Throughout time, God has called prophets and apostles who have guided me though some of my toughest fights and helped me see some of my greatest successes. The Book of Mormon was written by ancient prophets who lived on the American continent and had direct communication with God and testified of Christ. Here are a few of the things I've learned from the prophets of the Book of Mormon that have helped me weather the storms of life and experience success in growing closer to God:

Lehi

The words of Lehi are found at the beginning of the Book of Mormon. Lehi was a prophet and a descendant of Joseph of Egypt. He and his people dwelt among the tribe of Judah during the time of Jeremiah in the Old Testament, around 600 BC. Instructed of the Lord, Lehi and his people separated themselves from Judah in order to preserve a righteous branch of Israel during the Babylonian takeover. Lehi's account starts while he is in Jerusalem, but he and his people are instructed of God to build a ship and travel to the American continent.

In teaching his son Jacob, Lehi points out that men are instructed sufficiently that they know good from evil. In 2 Nephi 2:5 Lehi says, "And men are instructed sufficiently that they know good from evil. And the law is given unto men. And by the law no flesh is justified; or, by the law men are cut off. Yea, by the temporal law they were cut off; and also, by the spiritual law they perish from that which is good, and become miserable forever." Do all men really know good from evil? I believe they do.

I know there are moral principles we all have differing opinions on. There seems to be so much gray area in life that it can sometimes be hard to figure out what is right or wrong. But if we look at major acts of good and evil, the answer becomes obvious. Are we providing or stealing, helping or hurting? I believe that deep down we all understand the concept of good and evil, even if we call it by different names, like bringing happiness or bringing misery. Helping people brings feelings of peace and satisfaction; hurting people brings feelings of guilt, unease, and dissatisfaction.

Verse 5 also talks about how we are spiritually and temporally cut off from God because we have all made evil decisions. Remember that "birds of a feather" thing? We cannot dwell with a God who is perfect when we are so imperfect. We wouldn't feel comfortable in our fallen state with God. But we want to be with Him, knowing instinctively that we are His literal offspring. So what can we do? In verses 6 and 7 Lehi goes on to tell us the good news—a Messiah, full of grace and truth, will come to redeem us by offering Himself as a sacrifice for our sins to satisfy the law. Lehi testifies that Christ will sacrifice Himself for all those who have a broken hearts and contrite spirits. Remember the importance of realizing our nothingness before an all-powerful God? Now, 2 Nephi 2:10 says all men will be judged according to truth and holiness and by the law the Holy One has given. This perfect law demands that a punishment be affixed to the law that is broken; the punishment is in opposition to the happiness that is taken due to our sin. That makes the Atonement necessary. In 2 Nephi 2:11 we find the concept of opposition in all things: righteousness versus wickedness, holiness versus misery, good versus bad.

Opposition makes life possible. It reminds me of Newton's third law of motion: For every *action* there is an equal and opposite *reaction*.

We can prove Newton's third law of motion in our physical world, but could it also be true in a spiritual sense? Could there be an equal and opposite reaction to our spirits? Could good works propel our spirit forward in progression and evil works stop that progression or even cause us to move backward?

Good works are often demanding and difficult, and yet they leave us feeling better about ourselves. The *action* is hard, honest work, the *reaction* is feeling good; thus, we move in a positive direction, and long-term progression is achieved in spirit and body.

Evil works are often easy and fun at the time, yet they leave you feeling worse about yourself. The *action* is to lie, cheat, take advantage of others, and have fun. The *reaction* is feeling guilt and corruption of spirit and body. Thus, our progress is stopped.

Lehi also says all things must be a compound in one. He says in 2 Nephi 2:13 that "if there is no law, there is no sin. If there is no sin, there is no righteousness. If there is no righteousness, there is no happiness."

Let's look at it the opposite way. If there is no law, there is no sin. If there is no sin, there is no punishment. If there is no punishment, there is no misery.

I have experienced happiness, and I have experienced misery. I may not be able to prove it to you, but because you have also experienced happiness and misery, you can relate. You have been through similar situations, so you can completely understand and believe me, even though I can't prove my feelings to you.

Could our guilt and misery be evidence of the reality of God and His plan? Are moments of happiness a testimony of God's existence? In 2 Nephi 2:14, Lehi bears his testimony that God "created all things in heaven and in earth, both things to act and things to be acted upon." He goes on to say that when God created the world, He introduced our first parents to the forbidden fruit, and in opposition to that, He created the tree of life, one being sweet, the other being bitter (see verse 15). We see in verse 16 that God gives man agency, or the ability to choose. Having opposites allows us to choose. Lehi goes on to talk about how an angel fell from heaven and became the devil, having sought that which was evil (see verse 17). He then explains that it was this fallen angel, the devil, who wanted all humankind miserable like unto himself (see verse 18).

At the time, Adam and Eve had not yet eaten the forbidden fruit, therefore they had not sinned. (Without sin, there is no righteousness; it is opposition that makes the plan work.) They could choose the forbidden fruit, but they had not yet made the choice to eat it. Without having eaten the forbidden fruit, they remained the way God created them—without the ability to progress. If good was all you knew, could you really know the difference between good and bad?

In 2 Nephi 2:18, the devil tempts Eve to eat the forbidden fruit, using the logic if she does so, she will know good from evil. Adam and Eve both partake of the fruit and are cast out of the garden (see verse 19). We see them cast into a world of opposition, where they must now till the earth. Their survival now depends on their work, this life becoming a probationary period with a commandment to repent. Because of the transgression of Adam and Eve, we are lost.

That makes a lot of sense. Many people say we are born sinners because of Adam's transgression, but Lehi says we are born lost. He explains that if Adam had not transgressed and fallen, everything God created would have stayed in the same state forever and Adam and Eve would never have had children (see verse 22–23). He states, "Adam fell that men might be and men are that they might have joy" (verse 25). He also tells us that the Messiah came to redeem men from the fall, and because we are redeemed, we are free (see verse 26). We know good from evil and are free to act and not be acted upon. 2 Nephi 2:27 explains how we are free to choose liberty and eternal life or captivity and death. Lehi then testifies of a Mediator who will come, and then he urges Jacob to live the commandments. He also warns against choosing everlasting death by living according to the flesh. Lehi also expresses his love to his sons by telling them he has no other objective than the welfare of their souls.

Let's briefly summarize the important concepts we've learned in 2 Nephi 2:

> We all know right from wrong.
>
> We will be judged according to a perfect law.
>
> Punishment is affixed to the law that is broken.
>
> Opposition is the reason we can exist.
>
> Opposition exists in both the physical and spiritual worlds.
>
> God created all things to act or to be acted upon.
>
> God gave man agency, or the ability to choose.
>
> The angel who fell from heaven is the devil.
>
> You cannot know good if you do not know evil.
>
> Adam and Eve needed to partake of the fruit to have children.
>
> Because of Adam and Eve's transgression, we are born lost.
>
> The Messiah will redeem those who come to Him with a broken heart and contrite spirit.

When I read these words, the Holy Ghost testifies to me that I'm reading the words of a prophet. Lehi spent his life in service to God, raising his family in righteousness. It was his faith and obedience that prepared him for the responsibility of leading his family and kin to the New World and establishing the gospel in the Western Hemisphere.

I know Lehi is a prophet because his words bring enlightenment to my mind. In his testimony of God and the Messiah, I understand God and His plan as I have never before understood them. As I read Lehi's words, I am overwhelmed by the feeling that Lehi had no other objective than the welfare of our souls. Lehi's words are the words of a man who had regular communication with God throughout his long life. I know Lehi was a prophet of God because when I read his words, they bring me closer to God. I can't prove it, but I can feel it. Please read the words of Lehi and see if you experience the same.

Jacob

There are two things I know to be true. First, everyone will die. Second, when I do something wrong, I feel guilt. These two things—guilt and death—have weighed upon the human mind from the beginning of time. In 2 Nephi 9, Lehi's son Jacob starts out by telling us to rejoice, and then he explains why: we will all die, and that's part of the plan. He also tells us we are cut off from the Lord here on earth and that this is also part of the plan. It doesn't sound like good news, but it does bring some peace to know that death and separation from God are not incidental.

Jacob then talks about the Resurrection—the idea that our bodies will die and then be brought back to life and reunite with our spirits. He talks of a spiritual death brought on by transgression, or sin. Jacob points out there are two deaths—spiritual and physical—and that it is a combination of both that consigns us to hell. But Jacob also tells us to rejoice because of the Atonement. Jacob calls it an infinite Atonement and explains how it works. Jesus, the Creator of the world and the Son of God, came to earth in the flesh and suffered the pains of all men, women, and children. The Atonement satisfied the demands of the eternal laws. Remember, where there is a law, there must be a punishment, and with laws and punishments there comes justice. The Atonement satisfies the demands of justice; that's God's plan.

Jacob gives us instructions on how to apply the Atonement in our lives. Christ paid the price for our sins, and if we devote our lives to Christ through faith, repentance, and baptism, we will one day receive a perfected body through the Resurrection and a perfected spirit through the Atonement. That way, when we stand at the Final Judgment, we will be qualified to enter the kingdom of God. The Atonement satisfies the demands of justice, which was the plan from the beginning.

Jacob then tells us the plan of the evil one. It's the evil one's plan to take advantage of our foolishness. He tries to get us to think we are smarter than God and that we don't need God or His plan. Jacob warns us against sin and lets us know that even he, Jacob, is bound down by sin. We all need the saving grace of our Savior Jesus Christ—there are no exceptions. Toward the end of the chapter, Jacob testifies of the importance of constant prayer and reminds us of the covenant God made with Israel.

Jacob brings up some interesting points. God designed a plan with requirements for us to obtain eternal life. If we fulfill our part of the plan, Christ will fulfill His part. Jacob testifies that Christ will come to satisfy the demands of justice. I like Jacob's idea of law, justice, and satisfying demand. I have thought and been asked many times, "If God is so powerful, why does He not just bring us back to heaven—every one of us?" He could simply say, "Bring them back," and—bam—in a flash everyone He ever created would be standing in heaven with Him.

Why do we need to come to earth, and why do we need laws? Because we cannot just be handed greatness or be given physical or spiritual perfection.

As I write this, my mother is organizing a Pinewood Derby, or toy car race, for the Cub Scouts, ages eight to eleven years old. Each boy must build a small car, then race his car against the cars the other Scouts in his troop have built. About four cars will race at the same time. They are all timed as well, so not only can you see the race, you can also see the times, fastest to slowest.

Why do I bring this up? The whole point of the race is to give these boys a chance to learn how to build and to feel the joy of victory or the pain of defeat. If the boys pay attention to the rules and proven principles of success, with a little hard work, they can build a competition-worthy car and feel proud of their effort. If they are lazy and neglectful, they will find themselves struggling with the pains of defeat. At my first Pinewood Derby at age nine, I lost every race, every time. It hurt. As they presented me with the Best Sport Award, I did everything in my power to hold back my tears so my friends wouldn't see me cry.

Why don't they just give each boy a perfectly engineered car? Each car would likely get the same time. No one would lose, and no one would win; therefore, no one would have to feel the way I did. It was embarrassing. But the only way to feel the joy of victory is to know the agony of defeat. Hence the reason we are given laws. We can't just *be* winners; we need to *become* winners. In God's plan of redemption, there is room for error and room for improvement. We are not just factory-made heavenly beings. We must become heavenly beings by overcoming our imperfections. We are all different in countless ways. It's part of the plan for us to make mistakes that we might learn, grow, and overcome our weaknesses. Christ offered Himself so that when we failed, we could still qualify for eternal life with Heavenly Father.

Paying attention to the thoughts I have as I read the Book of Mormon helps me to know it is true. I've asked myself why we even have laws. Jacob answers that question. As I continue to read the Book of Mormon my mind is flooded with understanding. I truly feel I'm starting to see life the way God wants me to.

That's one of many things I have learned while reading the Book of Mormon. Try it. It's a fantastic read. Open your mind as you are reading, and I promise the Spirit will lead and guide you and teach you beyond your mortal comprehension.

I love Jacob chapter 4, verse 5, because it brings clarity to one of my favorite Bible stories, that of Abraham and his son Isaac. I'll be honest—there were times I thought it was somewhat crazy that God would ask Abraham to sacrifice Isaac. I've been a member of The Church of Jesus Christ of Latter-day Saints since I was eight. I've read the Book of Mormon many times, but it wasn't until recently I noticed how this verse brings clarity to the Abraham and Isaac story.

Jacob starts out by saying how all the prophets have believed in Christ and have worshiped the Father in the name of Christ. He also tells us that the law of Moses points us to Christ: "Even as it was accounted unto Abraham in the wilderness to be obedient unto the commands of God in offering up Isaac, which is a similitude of God and his Only Begotten Son" (Jacob 4:5). Jacob here teaches us that the account of Abraham and Isaac is a representation of God and His Son, Jesus Christ. Just as God was willing to sacrifice His Son to satisfy the demands of the law, Abraham was willing to sacrifice his son to satisfy the commandments of God. Jacob tells us it's a "similitude," or, in other words, it was similar.

Abraham was put in a situation similar to God's. The Father was willing to send his perfect Only Begotten Son to this evil, fallen world where Christ would be sacrificed to save all of the Father's imperfect children. Abraham had only one son, Isaac, with his wife, Sarah. As God was willing to sacrifice His Son, Abraham was willing to sacrifice Isaac to keep the commandments. And the result? Given the pain and agony Abraham must have felt in having to offer up his beloved Isaac, imagine the joy he was able to experience at the opposite end of the spectrum, when he'd passed the test of obedience and was sent a ram to be sacrificed instead of Isaac.

Just as those Scouts had to put in the work and follow the guidelines in order to experience the joy of success with the derby, when we are obedient to God and do our best to keep His commandments, we will experience the joy of success in our endeavors. Doctrine and Covenants 130:20–21 reads: "There is a law irrevocably decreed in heaven before the foundations of this world, upon which all blessings are predicated—And when we obtain any blessing from God, it is by obedience to that law upon which it is predicated." Think of that promise as you contemplate the story of Abraham and Isaac. I believe it was obedience to God's commandments that qualified Abraham to be tied to God through the Abrahamic Covenant. Simply put, God and Christ have a perfect love for us, and that perfect love is what brings Them power over all things. That love is what brought life to the human race. On that same note, Abraham and Isaac exercised obedience to the commandments of God. Abraham and Isaac's obedience to God in all things was a representation of God's and Christ's willingness to do all thing for us. Obedience is what binds Abraham and his seed to God through a covenant (see Genesis 22:9–18). Abraham's willingness to sacrifice Isaac satisfied the law—obedience to God in all things.

God wanted to pour out blessings upon the entire human family, and it was obedience in the most extreme case that qualified Abraham to bring these blessings to His children: "And in thy seed shall all the nations of the earth be blessed because thou hast obeyed my voice" (Genesis 22:18). Now, remember Doctrine and Covenants 130:20: "There is a law irrevocably decreed in heaven before the foundation of this world, upon which all blessings are predicated." For God to offer blessings to all His children, He needed a prophet to come to earth, a man willing to be obedient to His commands at all costs. As I read the words of Jacob concerning Abraham, my mind begins to overflow with understanding, and I'm reminded of other scriptures that increase this understanding. This gives me greater motivation to take the name of Christ upon me and to stay true to the covenants, or promises, I have made to God through baptism. Not only have Jacob's words helped me understand the significance of Abraham and Isaac and the reality of Jacob as a Book of Mormon prophet, but they've reminded me of what God and Jesus have done for us and how They want to bless us. And, more importantly, they've brought me closer to Them.

Enos

Enos was a prophet who lived on the American continent in about 420 BC. The words of Enos have always been special to me. Though his account is brief, his message has helped me see how true disciples of Christ act. Enos tells us of the wrestle he had with God as he was hunting: "And I will tell you of the wrestle which I had before God" (Enos 1:2). As a wrestler and a hunter myself, I was drawn to Enos's words.

Why would he use the word *wrestle*? The word *wrestle* is also used in Genesis 32:24, which scripture talks about how Jacob, the son of

Isaac, wrestled all night until the breaking of day, demanding a blessing of safety from his angry brother Esau. Jacob's wrestling match was so fierce his hip was dislocated, but when the Lord saw Jacob's conviction and perseverance in requesting blessings, He changed Jacob's name to Israel, which, translated from Hebrew is a two-part word derived from *Yisra-El*, or "wrestle God." So why is the term *wrestle* used in the texts regarding Enos and Jacob? It's my belief that the word is used to show the extreme lengths these to prophets were willing to go to obtain the blessings they sought.

When I wrestle in competition, right after my match, I'm often exhausted to the point where I'm on the ground, gasping for air, my lungs burning. Water does not make me feel any better because drinking water at that point makes me feel like throwing up. I've pushed my body to its physical limit. Do I want the Lord's blessings to the same degree I want to win a wrestling match? How far am I willing to push myself spiritually to obtain the Lord's blessings? Jacob and Enos are great examples of pushing their souls to the limit to secure the Lord's blessings.

Jacob's first concern was for his people. He believed his twin brother Esau and the house of Esau were coming to take over the house of Jacob. Jacob and Esau were in constant competition for their father's (Isaac) birthright, even as they lay in their mother's (Rebekah) womb. Esau was born first, which qualified him for the birthright, but two times Jacob was able to step in and take the birthright from him. The first time, Esau sold his birthright to Jacob for a mess of pottage (see Genesis 25). The second, Rebekah assisted Jacob in receiving the birthright from Isaac while Esau was away hunting. This led Esau to say within his heart, "The days of mourning for my father are at hand; then will I slay my brother Jacob" (Genesis 27:41).

Here we see why Jacob would wrestle with God so fervently in prayer for blessings. As head patriarch, Jacob was responsible for the welfare and safety of a large following that consisted of his family, workers, and kin. Jacob's messengers returned with news that Esau was headed their way with four hundred men. That message struck fear in Jacob's heart and prompted him to pray. Later that night, as Jacob sought a bit of solitude to contemplate his fate, the Lord confronted him. It is here that we learn that Jacob wrestled with the Lord and begged the Lord to protect his people. He prayed with such passion that it turned to wrestling.

The Lord wants to bless us when we are trying to help others and are willing to do what it takes to qualify for His blessings. Jacob sets a powerful example of doing whatever is necessary to secure the Lord's blessing for others.

Enos did the same. As he was out hunting, the words of his father concerning eternal life were brought to his mind. He kneels down and begins to pray mightily. Enos's prayer—heartfelt, emotional, long, and exhausting—lasts through the day and into the night, which is why he calls it a wrestle before God.

One difference between Enos's wrestle with God and Jacob's wrestle with God is that Enos prays for his own soul. The nature of the prayer and Enos's faith in Christ qualify him to receive a remission of his sins. What happens next is the best part: "Now it came to pass that when I had heard these words I began to feel a desire for the welfare of my brethren, the Nephites: wherefore, I did pour out my whole soul unto God for them" (Enos 1:9). When people turn to God, they naturally turn toward God's children. Jacob turned to God in order to help his people. Enos turned to God in order to find God. Then, once he found Him, he became concerned with the welfare of others. When I found God, I also felt a desire for the welfare those around me, and I poured out my soul to God to bless and protect my loved ones.

When you understand the greatness of God and recognize your own unworthiness before Him, you will be compelled to plead for forgiveness. In these moments of prayer, when you feel God's greatness and His love for you, and you experience His forgiveness and the peace and joy that come with it, your heart will naturally turn to others. And when you concern yourself with the welfare of others, you know you are truly converted to Christ, as it is His only desire to save us and bring us back to the Father.

Another example of this type of transformation is that of Saul, who, once he was converted to Christ, his name was changed to Paul. He then spent the remainder of his days teaching of Christ. Although my faith in Christ does not compare with the great prophets, such as Israel, Enos, and Paul, in my most heartfelt prayers, I can feel the presence of the Lord through the Holy Ghost. When I understand how much God loves me and that He has provided a way for me to return to live with Him through Christ, even though I offer Him nothing, my soul is filled with an indescribable joy, and I cannot wait to share that joy with the people in my life. Seeing these great prophets experience the same motivation I experience as I learn of God convinces me I have found the same God as Abraham, Isaac, Jacob, Enos and Paul.

King Benjamin

King Benjamin was a prophet who lived on the American continent in about 124 BC. The words from the speech he gave to his people are found in the Book of Mormon, starting in Mosiah 1. After King Benjamin finished speaking, the multitude fell to the earth in fear because they now understood that they were less than the dust of the earth. They begged for mercy through the atoning blood of the Savior (see Mosiah 4:1–2).

King Benjamin reminds us to keep in remembrance the greatness of God and our nothingness and to call on His name every day (see verse 11). He says that if we pray daily, we will be filled with love and retain a remission of our sins, which will lead us to gaining a knowledge of God and His glory (verse 12). In verses 15 through 17, King Benjamin talks about the importance of love, charity, and service. He then informs us in verses 19 through 21 that we are all beggars because we all depend on God for our lives and for our substance.

There was a time when I was filled with pride and believed all my success was a result of *my* hard work. But, like King Benjamin's people,

I have been brought down into the depths of humility as I've realized God's greatness and how I am nothing without my Creator. As I realize I'm nothing, I understand that all I have comes from God. I also know that as I pray daily, I feel His love for me despite my nothingness. God's love for me in spite of my own nothingness motivates me to serve and help others, knowing I am also a beggar. His teachings help me realize how all things are made possible through God's plan. King Benjamin points out a humbling truth. That knowledge testifies to me that King Benjamin was a prophet called of God.

Abinadi

The story about Abinadi is also found in the book of Mosiah. This prophet lived on the American continent around 148 BC. Something you may want to ask yourself as you read the Book of Mormon and Bible is how you can apply these stories and teachings in your life. When I first read the teachings of Abinadi, I merely saw them as history. But as I continued to read them, I realized he was actually talking to this generation—to me personally. The key is to look for how the text is meaningful to you.

When I first read Mosiah 11:20–21, it seemed Abinadi was strictly talking to wicked King Noah and his people. I just couldn't see how this message applied to me, but then as I read between the lines, I came to realize that Abinadi's words speak to this generation as well.

> 20 . . . Wo be unto this people, for I have seen their abominations, and their wickedness, and their whoredoms; and except they repent I will visit them in mine anger.
>
> 21 And except they repent and turn to the Lord their God, behold, I will deliver them into the hands of their enemies; yea, and they shall be brought into bondage; and they shall be afflicted by the hand of their enemies.

Let's take a look at the same verses, changing some of the words so we can see how they apply to us:

20 Wo be unto [you], for I have seen [your] abominations, and [your] wickedness, and [your] whoredoms; and except [you] repent I will visit [you] in mine anger.

21 And except [you] repent and turn to the Lord [your] God, behold, I will deliver [you] into the hands of [your] enemies; yea, and [you] shall be brought into bondage; and [you] shall be afflicted by the hand of [your] enemies.

When you look at it like this, it's quite sobering. It almost makes you rethink who God is. Throughout most of this book, we've been talking about a God of love, mercy, and forgiveness. These verses in Mosiah seem to focus on His wrath. When we think about King Benjamin's words regarding our being unworthy creatures and that our existence is totally dependent on God, you can see why God's anger is kindled against us when we sin, because what sin really amounts to is pride, which is synonymous with ingratitude and saying we know better than God.

Let's take another look at these verses and further adapt them for our day:

20 . . . Wo be unto [you], for I have seen [your obsessions], and [your passions], and [your addictions]; and except [you] repent I will visit [you] in mine anger.

21 And except [you] repent and turn to the Lord [your] God, behold, I will deliver [you] into the hands of [your addictions]; yea, and [you] shall be brought into bondage; and [you] shall be afflicted by [your desires].

Here, we are being counseled to repent and told that if we do, the Lord will have mercy on us. We are also being told that if we do not repent, our sins become bad habits that turn into addictions and that these addictions become the enemy that holds us in bondage. It is bondage to addiction that brings sorrow to the soul. The resulting sorrow, bondage, and affliction are not a curse from God; we bring them upon ourselves when we turn from God. "I, the Lord, am bound when ye do what I say; but when ye do not what I say, ye have no promise." (Doctrine and Covenants 82:10)

Sometimes we have to search, ponder, and pray to understand the deeper meaning of certain passages, but some are literal. For instance, if you continue to read the words of Abinadi, he preaches the Ten Commandments, the same Ten Commandments Moses introduced (Mosiah 13). The Ten Commandments are quite literal. Most are "Thou shalt nots," though two give advice on things we *should* do—keeping the Sabbath holy and honoring our fathers and mothers. The Ten Commandments are exactly that—commandments that are easy to understand. They are a list of dos and don'ts and are pretty straightforward. I'm sure that is why they are so popular.

But much like the Savior's parables in the New Testament, there are passages of scripture we have to work at to find the deeper meaning. Abinadi's teachings are chock-full of truths that are ours for a little effort.

The advice I personally received from Abinadi is to avoid habit-forming substances. My ability to avoid addiction has been one of my greatest tools in finding God. It's a simple fact: if your mind is obsessed with satisfying your addictions, it's hard to find time to find God. The first two commandments are: "Thou shalt have no gods before me" and "Thou shalt not make unto thee any graven images. Thou shalt not bow down thyself to them." Whether you're worshiping a drug, pornography, or a golden calf, the result is the same. Anything that puts you in bondage keeps you away from God.

Alma the Younger

Alma's father, Alma the Elder, initially a wicked man, heard the words of Abinadi in person, was converted to Christ, and became a prophet. Ironically, his son Alma the Younger rebelled against God and persecuted the Church. Alma the Younger had a unique conversion to Christ. It began with an angel sent from the Lord to Alma and his four friends, the sons of Mosiah, who were also rebellious.

Alma was struck dumb and couldn't move for two days and two nights as the angel visited him. After Alma was converted to Christ, he became a missionary and prophet. We can read his words to the people of Zarahemla: "Have ye spiritually been born of God? Have ye experienced this mighty change in your hearts?" (Alma 5:14). It's as if he is saying that when you are born of God, you experience a mighty change of heart.

Alma often taught with questions. Read Alma 5, and let these questions settle on your mind. Many godly principles are taught by simply asking questions. Much of my conversion came because I had questions and thought about these questions often. The simple truths of the gospel that came in answer to my questions have been a great guide for me in my conversion to Christ. Let me again share with you some of the questions that led to my conversion.

Is there a God?

What does God expect of me?

How will God communicate with me?

Why do I feel guilty when I take advantage of others or hurt others?

Is guilt evidence of God's existence?

How do I feel when I help others?

Are these good feelings during service God's way of communicating with me?

If God exists, have my previous sins disqualified me from His presence?

Am I condemned to hell?

Why would God create us then condemn us to hell?

Do we need a Redeemer?

Is Christ our Redeemer?

Why do I feel peace when I learn of Christ?

Why do I feel peace when I act like Christ?

In chapter 5, Alma asks us a number of thought-provoking, soul-stirring questions:

> 14 ... Have ye spiritually been born of God? Have ye received his image in your countenance? Have ye experienced this mighty change in your hearts?
>
> 15 Do ye exercise faith in the redemption of him who created you? Do you look forward with an eye of faith, and view this mortal body raised in immortality, and this corruption raised in incorruption, to stand before God to be judged according to the deeds which have been done in the mortal body?
>
> 16 I say unto you, can you imagine to yourself that ye hear the voice of the Lord, saying unto you, in that day; Come unto me ye blessed, for behold, your works have been works of righteousness upon the face of the earth?
>
> 17 Or do ye imagine to yourselves that ye can lie unto the Lord in that day, and say—Lord, our works have been righteous works upon the face of the earth—and that he will save you?
>
> 18 Or otherwise, can ye imagine yourselves brought before the tribunal of God with your souls filled with guilt and remorse, having a remembrance of all your guilt, yea, a perfect remembrance of all your wickedness, yea, a remembrance that ye have set at defiance the commandments of God?
>
> 19 I say unto you, can ye look up to God at that day with a pure heart and clean hands? I say unto you, can you look up, having the image of God engraven upon your countenances?
>
> 20 I say unto you, can ye think of being saved when you have yielded yourselves to become subject to the devil?"

In Alma 12, we learn of Zeezrom, a wicked man who attempted to use words and money to destroy the faith of the believers. Here, again, Alma teaches us with questions. We see in Alma 12 how those questions are an effective check for Zeezrom, who begins to suffer when he realizes how wrong he's been. Zeezrom understands he has been caught in his lies before God, and he trembles under a consciousness of his guilt.

In Zeezrom's experience, I see the nature of our pain as we will be brought to stand before Christ at our judgment. I believe that if we aren't in alignment with God, we will "tremble more exceedingly, for [we will be] convinced more and more of the power of God" (Alma 12:7).

The questions asked in Alma 5 cause me to contemplate my sins and the power of my Creator. In Alma 12, I get to put myself in the shoes of Zeezrom and understand the pain of everlasting shame. But also I feel the glory and relief brought through God's mercy as I understand I can repent through the Lord Jesus Christ.

Alma the Younger's teachings have convinced me that redemption can come through Christ no matter what our situation is. I love Alma's testimony of how he came to know Christ (see Alma 5:44–46) because I can do the same. He informs us his knowledge of God and Christ came through prayer and fasting and the power of the Holy Ghost. I have also fasted and prayed and have been taught by the power of the Holy Ghost. When I see Alma learn of God in a similar way, it tells me the God of Alma is the one true God, the same God I've discovered and the same God discovered by the prophets of old.

Nephi, Son of Helaman

In Helaman 7, Nephi is pointing out the wickedness of the people in about 23–21 BC. There are a few things that testify to me that Nephi was a prophet of God. First, he wrestled with God in prayer for the benefit of others, as did Jacob and Enos. But unlike Jacob and Enos, he did not call it a wrestle. He described it as pouring out his soul unto God as he mourned for the wickedness of the people. He never used the word *wrestle*, but to me it sounds as if he was wrestling with God in prayer for the Nephite people. Struggling with God in prayer on behalf of others is a telltale sign that someone is converted to Christ and is working for Him.

Nephi asks the people, "How could you have forgotten your God?" (Helaman 7:20–21). He tells them it is because they have set their minds on the praise of men and on acquiring riches. When life becomes easy through riches and comforts, we often forget the Lord. This can happen personally or collectively and is known as the "pride cycle." Throughout time people have gone through cycles where they lift themselves up in pride and turn from the Lord because of their success and riches. People who do not need the Lord quickly forget Him. One challenge we face in life is continuing to turn toward the Lord when things are going well. People often turn to Him in the midst of tragedy, such as death, disease, natural disasters, or war. In these times we understand our weakness and dependence on God's grace. But in times of prosperity, it's easy to convince ourselves we are happy and successful because we are smart, talented, strong, and capable of solving our problems. In the course of human history, we see this cycle repeated again and again on both a large and small scale, but the only pride cycle you can control is your own. Turn to the Lord in your successes as well as in your challenges.

The Nephites are also caught up in murdering, plundering, stealing, lying, and all manner of evil, and Nephi calls them to repentance. In Helaman 7, he uses the word *repent* nine times. A common pattern I see with prophets is that they preach repentance. Nephi taught repentance to the Nephites on the American continent about 23–21 BC, but Moroni added the words of Nephi to the Book of Mormon in about AD 400. Moroni saw in a vision our day and knew of the pride of our hearts (see Mormon 8:34–41). Thus, the teachings of Nephi are written for our day. We cannot force the world to repent, but we can prepare ourselves to meet God through individual repentance.

Though I am far from perfect, I have done my best to follow the advice of Nephi and have humbled myself and made repentance a common practice in my life. I regularly ask for forgiveness. This constant repentance process has brought me closer to God. I know repentance can bring all people closer to God in this life and bind them to

God in the next. It's my peace of mind through repentance in Christ's name that has convinced me Nephi was a prophet called to testify of Jesus Christ.

Jesus Christ

Christ is not only a prophet like Lehi, Alma, and Abinadi, but He is the central figure of the Book of Mormon and the reason it was written. Christ visited the American continent around AD 34–35, after His death and Resurrection in Jerusalem. In 3 Nephi 9, we see Christ preparing the way for His coming on the American continent. What we read there is that disaster covers the land. Then the voice of Christ is heard throughout the land. Christ proclaims repentance and then testifies of His power and notifies the people that He has destroyed many cities because of their wickedness: "Zarahemla have I burned . . . Moroni have I caused to be sunk . . . Moronihah have I covered with earth. . . . Gilgal have I caused to be sunk" (3 Nephi 9:3–6).

And the list goes on. I always wondered why a loving God would allow so much destruction before His coming. But when I start to understand the Bible and the Book of Mormon and see God's relationship with mankind, it starts to make sense why destruction would precede Christ coming to the Nephites and Lamanites in the Americas. Let me explain. The name Israel refers to Christ's covenant people. The tribe we know of in the time of Christ is the tribe of Judah. They were found in Jerusalem. The Nephites and Lamanites were from the house of Israel, but descended through the tribe of Joseph, and came to the American continent.

We have two records of Israelite tribes in the time of Christ. We know from the Bible that Christ was born into the tribe of Judah, and we know from the Book of Mormon that Christ visited the tribe of Joseph. These tribes had prophets and knew Christ was coming, yet they still lived in sin and would not repent. We learn of Christ being born in Bethlehem and ministering in Jerusalem while in a mortal body and living among sinners. Though He was kind and loving to sinners, He had to subject Himself to them to fulfill His responsibilities as a Savior. Christ needed to be sacrificed as a Lamb *by* sinners *for* sinners. He fulfilled this responsibility and subjected Himself to the will of evil men. As a God in a mortal body, He came to earth and allowed Himself to be mocked, spit on, and tortured. But that was part of the responsibility He took upon Himself in carrying out God's plan of happiness. After the Atonement, Crucifixion, and Resurrection, Christ was no longer a God with a mortal body. He was now a God with a perfect, resurrected body. His time of suffering was over. He was now a God and joint-heir with God the Father, both in body and spirit. He had attained dominion over all things, both spiritual and physical, through His power and priesthood.

Now it was time for Christ to visit His other covenant people, the descendants of Joseph, or the Nephites and the Lamanites. When the Savior finished ministering to the Saints in Jerusalem, He went and ministered in the Americas among the Nephites and Lamanites. When Christ went to the Americas, He did not come as a sacrifice as in Jerusalem. He came as a God, with power over all things. Because He came as a God, He could not visit those who would mock Him, spit upon Him or question His authority. The time for the unrepentant sinner to exercise power over Christ was past. Christ came to the Americas as an all-powerful God having already fulfilled the role of a humble Lamb. Only those willing to repent and worship Christ were left as survivors of the destruction in the Americas.

In 3 Nephi 9:22, after the destruction, Christ communicates in a way that all in the land can hear Him. He commands the people to repent and come unto Him. Then, in 3 Nephi 10:12, Christ informs them that it is the more righteous people who have been saved. He also defines who the righteous are and informs them why they have been saved. Those who have been saved are the people who did not stone the prophets or shed the blood of the Saints. Of course, Christ would not appear to a people who would challenge Him and His authority or a people who would attempt to stone Him. The people of Christ were people of common courtesy who respected others.

While the people are conversing about the changes in the land and about Christ and the sign of His death, they hear a voice and are visited by the Savior:

> And it was not a harsh voice, neither was it a loud voice; nevertheless, and notwithstanding it being a small voice it did pierce them that did hear to the center, insomuch that there was no part of their frame that did not cause to quake; yea, it did pierce them to the very soul, and it did cause their hearts to burn. (3 Nephi 11:3)

> They saw a man descending out of heaven; and He was clothed in a white robe and He came down and stood in the midst of them. (3 Nephi 11:8)

> Behold I am Jesus Christ, whom the prophets testified shall come to the world. (3 Nephi 11:10)

The Book of Mormon is another testament of Jesus Christ. When you read the Bible, you are conditioning your mind to find Christ. From its first verse ("In the beginning God created the heaven and the earth," Genesis 1:1) to its last ("The grace of our Lord Jesus Christ be with you all Amen," Revelation 22:21), and on every page in between, we are preparing our minds to know the Creator and Savior of the world.

As we read the Old Testament, we see the way our Savior and Creator dealt with the people and prophets of old. The Old Testament prepares us to recognize the Christ of the New Testament. One could read the New Testament and see it as merely a good story. But if you read and study the Old Testament prior to reading the New Testament, you will see the New Testament in a new light. The Old Testament teaches of Christ through metaphors and direct prophecies. When you see Jesus Christ introduced in the New Testament, you know through the Old Testament that this is the Savior prophesied for thousands of years.

With a strong understanding of the Old Testament, the New Testament is no longer just a good story. It becomes life-changing. Reading of Christ and *knowing* He is your Creator and Savior is different than reading of Christ and *wondering* if He is your Creator and Savior. If you have built an image of the Savior in your mind through consistent study of the Old Testament, the Christ of the New Testament will become the Living Christ to you. This new understanding of Christ and who He was before He was a mortal will help you recognize Him as a mortal. Then, when you understand how Christ functioned as the God of the Old Testament, you can recognize Him as a mortal in the New Testament.

The understanding I gained of Christ through reading the Old and New Testaments helped me to recognize Christ as the same glorified, resurrected God in the Book of Mormon.

When you see it in this light, you can see the ministry of Christ in His premortal life as Jehovah. This helps us understand Christ's ministry as a mortal as well as His post-Resurrection ministry. When you understand Christ through studying His premortal existence, earthly existence, and existence as a resurrected being, you are preparing yourself to meet Christ as you stand before Him at your judgment.

One day you will meet Jesus Christ face-to-face. Will you recognize Him? The scriptures are here to help you do that. Throughout history, people have been introduced to Christ and His messengers. When Christ and His message were not recognized, the blessed opportunity of knowing Christ was lost. Noah was called by Christ to be a prophet, and those who mocked him lost their lives in a flood. Moses was called by Christ, but when the people lifted their voices against Moses, they were bitten by serpents and died. When the Israelites turned to Moses, he provided a way for them to be saved. He made a brass serpent and raised it on a pole. All those who looked to Moses and the brass serpent were saved. The house of Israel was left for dead, yet they found safety in Christ through Moses. Moses was not their Savior, but he was called to save them from Egypt and the serpents.

These metaphors in the Old Testament remind us that even God's chosen people needed to be saved from both spiritual and physical death. Many prophets were called to prophesy of the coming of Christ. When Christ was born to Mary and Joseph, many of the people were not familiar with the scriptures or sayings of the prophets or had misinterpreted them and consequently missed out on the opportunity of knowing the Savior. Christ was born to the world as a humble baby, grew to be a perfect man who was sacrificed for the sins of the world. Those who understood the true nature of God through scriptures and prophets recognized the humble baby as the prophesied Savior. There were many humble people who were blessed to interact with Jesus during His mortal ministry. But there were others who had neglected the prophets and scriptures who, even when they came face-to-face with Jesus, did not recognize Him as the God of the Old Testament.

Before Christ came as a resurrected God to the Nephites and Lamanites, He cleansed the land of all those who would not receive Him or who would challenge Him. He also required repentance for all those who remained alive so they would be worthy to be in His presence. He then established His Church by calling a prophet, Nephi. Jesus gave Nephi the authority to baptize in His name. Christ also called twelve disciples and gave them authority to teach and baptize in His name. Christ also blessed the sick and afflicted as well as the children.

As I read the account of the Savior in the Book of Mormon, I know that this Jesus is the Jehovah of the Old Testament and the Christ of the New Testament. These three testaments of Christ carry the same message and spirit:

1. We may not recognize Christ if we do not study and seek after Him.
2. No matter what, we are all dependent on Christ and cannot be saved without Him.

3. We must be humble and attune ourselves to the Spirit of Christ so when we are presented with His scriptures, the words of His prophets, or even Christ Himself, we will recognize Him as our Creator, Savior, and Resurrected Lord.

The Book of Mormon is another testament of Jesus Christ. By reading it, I am preparing myself to meet my Savior.

Joseph Smith

Was Joseph Smith a prophet? Did Joseph Smith have regular communication with God? Did Joseph Smith communicate with the same Christ who communicated with Adam, Noah, Abraham, Isaac, and Jacob? If you want to know if Joseph Smith was a true prophet and was in regular communication with God, read the Book of Mormon. Joseph Smith translated it when he was twenty-three years old. He had no notes during the translation, other than the plates the ancient prophet Moroni gave him. Joseph had only three years of formal education, yet the Book of Mormon is written in perfect sequence, with no dates or events that are mismatched. Each book within it transitions flawlessly from prophet to prophet, people to people, and battle to battle.

The Book of Mormon is a 531-page book with 268,163 words, not including chapter summaries and footnotes. Joseph Smith translated the Book of Mormon in about sixty-five working days.

Let's compare that to this book, *Fighting to Find God*. This book was written by me, Eric Wahlin, between the time I was thirty-two to thirty-four. I constantly referred to my notes and checked my facts against internet sources. Even with these tools, I'm sure I made a few mistakes. I have thirteen years of formal education. Mine is a book with 54,945 words and took me 82,560 minutes to write. That's solid working time on a modern computer; the Book of Mormon was written with pen and ink in the eighteen hundreds. Let's break it down: 82,560 minutes is 1,376 hours, which is fifty-seven days. But that's fifty-seven days twenty-four hours a day. If you add in sleep and daily activities, the most I could work on this book would be four hours a day.

At four hours a day, it would have taken me 344 days to write. That's almost a year at four hours a day, every day.

I worked on my book for two years. Joseph Smith worked on the Book of Mormon for about three months. I wrote *Fighting to Find God*, taking the principles I used to become successful in fighting and comparing them to the principles I used to become successful in discovering God. It's a simple concept, really.

What Joseph Smith did was amazing. Is the Book of Mormon a simple story Joseph Smith dictated to someone who wrote it all down within sixty-five days? Let me share with you what I've discovered concerning the extraordinary, exact, and complex details of the Book of Mormon.

On my mission, when I was about twenty years old, I was asked a question about the Book of Mormon I did not know the answer to. I don't remember the question, but I do remember it was a simple question and that I should have known the answer. As a missionary it was my job to share the Book of Mormon with those I met. I had been in the mission field for a year. Being the senior companion, I had more experience, and it was my job to answer the tough questions. That was the problem. This was not a tough question. I should have known the answer. At the time, we were given two hours a day to study, and the fact that I didn't know the answer to a simple question was absolutely embarrassing. I resolved to learn everything I could about the Book of Mormon. But how? I was already studying it two hours a day.

That's when it hit me. I could make a Book of Mormon diagram. Sure, people had already made Book of Mormon diagrams. Why didn't I just look at those? Well, I already had a Book of Mormon diagram, and I still had a limited knowledge of the book. Obviously a diagram made by someone else was not enough. I needed my own so not only would I know the information, I would know where it came from. If I couldn't remember information during a lesson, I would have my own diagram. I would know exactly how to read it and where to find the information.

Once I resolved to learn more and to make a diagram, I spent every morning for the next three months with about twenty papers spread out on my desk, dresser, bed, and hanging on my walls. On top of those papers, I had multiple copies of the Book of Mormon opened to different pages. I also had several Bibles open to ensure that the dates of the Book of Mormon were in sync with those of the Bible. Here is the diagram I created while on my mission.

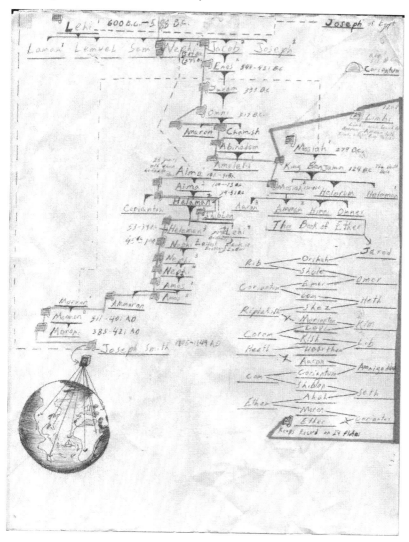

It may not look like much or make a lot of sense to you, but what I discovered while I was making this chart is that the Book of Mormon is complex, with many moving parts. The following are some examples of that complexity.

The Book of Mormon's dates needed to correspond with the Bible's dates. The Book of Mormon had three groups of people leaving the Old World and coming to the American continent—the Jaredites around 2300 BC, the Nephites around 588 BC, and the Mulekites shortly after the Nephites. These three groups of people mixed, divided, and warred with one with another. That's complicated by itself. The Book of Mormon also mentions when people were born, when they had kids, when they passed the records to the next generation, and when they died. It took a lot of patience as I struggled to find connections from people to people, prophet to prophet, and the records passing from one person to another. I checked the timelines to see if all the dates matched up. The Book of Mormon also mentions city placement—a city's direction and distance and characteristics. With all these moving parts and variables, the remarkable thing is that everything lines up.

Creating the diagram did two things for me. First, I achieved my goal of understanding the Book of Mormon better. Second, I was now totally convinced Joseph Smith was called by God to be a prophet and to translate the Book of Mormon. He established Christ's Church on the earth in the latter days, along with His authority, the priesthood. Christ is gathering His lost covenant tribes and building temples and binding families to Him through temple work. Christ is working with us in our day. And ever since the Church was established through Joseph Smith, Christ has guided us through His prophets.

Russell M. Nelson is the current prophet. The peace I feel when I read my scriptures, say my prayers, and serve others is the same peace I feel when I hear Russell M. Nelson speak. That feeling of peace testifies to me he is called by Christ to be our prophet today.

The Church of Jesus Christ is alive and well today. It started with Adam and then moved from generation to generation to Noah,

Abraham, Isaac, Jacob, Moses, and King David. Then Christ Himself came to minister among the people of Jerusalem. After Christ ministered to the tribes of Judah and Joseph around AD 34, the gospel of Christ was established by Christ, but shortly thereafter, the authority Christ established on the earth was lost when the Apostles were killed, one by one, by an increasingly wicked people who rejected the truths He had taught. For years, men lived in a state of ignorance and confusion regarding religious truths, oppressed by men who refused to give the general populace access to the Bible.

Then, through the American Revolution, freedom of religion was restored, and technology catapulted man into a new age where religious information was readily accessible to the people. Christ reestablished His Church in a time when it could be brought to all nations. He called Joseph Smith as a prophet in 1820. Joseph then translated the Book of Mormon and called apostles and elders to carry out the work of teaching and baptizing.

The work of baptizing in Christ's name is still going forward today under Christ's authority. Today God works through Russell M. Nelson and other Church leadership to do His work.

A Fighter's Promise

Can you imagine a fighter hoping to find success by merely hearing the words of his coach and then doing nothing? I can't. That fighter must take what he's learned and get up and drill it again and again, putting it into practice, testing it, and refining it so he can use it in a way that helps him become the best fighter he can be.

I have included many scriptures in this book, but this last scripture—Moroni 10:3–5—I'm not going to quote here. I want you to open the pages of the Book of Mormon and read it for yourself. The whole goal of this book is to help you know how to be more effective and successful in your fight to find God and, as a result, ultimate happiness. The Book of Mormon is the most powerful weapon you can use against doubt, discouragement, disappointment—anything the adversary will try to throw at you as you walk into the biggest fight of your life—the fight between good and evil, the fight for your soul. As you read it, you'll hear the voice of your Coach cutting through the noise and the distractions, and if you'll listen and do what He is telling you to do, you will be victorious in finding God. So please put this book down and read the Book of Mormon.

Bonus Material
Developing Structure to Achieve Your Fighting Goals

THIS SECTION IS FOR THOSE interested in fighting techniques. Because fighting is actually quite complex and can quickly become chaotic, all successful fighters must develop structure and a strong work ethic.

To experience any success in the midst of chaos, you need structure and a sense of direction. As you reflect on the importance of structure when it comes to fighting, consider how success in life is also based on having a structured plan. Fighting is chaos, and so is life. And much like structure and order promote success in fighting, they also promote success in finding God.

It's critical to have a plan in attaining your fighting goals. In chapter 1 we talked about the fundamentals of fighting. This chapter goes more in depth about the techniques of fighting—striking, wrestling, submission grappling, and ground and pound. I would like to add one more technique to the list: mixing arts, or techniques. Mixing the fighting arts is not something that comes naturally to a fighter. Even though mixing these arts can be difficult, if done right, you can make yourself one dangerous fighter who can bounce flawlessly from art to art without missing a beat. Mixing arts allows you to have the maximum potential in all positions.

Striking

There are ten major strikes that can be used while you and your opponent are about an arm's length apart, give or take a few inches.

- Jab
- Cross
- Lead hook
- Rear hook
- Lead uppercut
- Rear uppercut
- Lead front kick
- Rear front kick
- Lead roundhouse kick
- Rear roundhouse kick

You can use each strike in many different ways, and each strike has its own list of correct movements. The first thing you need to do is learn the ten strikes and then the correct movements for each strike. Each strike has a different range. For example, with a rear front kick, I'm using my rear leg. I like to use my rear front kick when my lead foot is about three feet away from my opponent's lead foot; that's the right distance for a rear front kick. For a rear hook, I'm using the hand on the rear side of my stance. I like to use the rear hook when I'm close and my lead foot is near the same level as my opponent's lead foot or when our feet are almost touching and I'm right up next to my opponent.

The next range is body to body or chest to chest—or right up in each other's faces. When you are close fighting like this, you need to use different strikes—mostly knees and elbows. There are many different types of knees and elbows, all of which have lists of proper movements.

The last set of strikes I will mention are long-range strikes, meaning you and your opponent are more than three feet away from each other.

The strikes you will want to use at this range are a turning side kick and side kick. The side kick is just what it sounds like—you turn your body to the side and kick your opponent. The turning side kick is a bit more powerful than the simple side kick because you add a turning motion to create more power. As your body turns a full circle, you generate power that transfers into the kick. You can use these two kicks many different ways, each kick, again, having a list of proper movements. To be a good MMA fighter, you need to perfect these strikes in addition to the ten already mentioned.

There are more strikes I haven't mentioned, but these are a great starting point and constitute most of the strikes used in stand-up fighting. I always advise fighters to start training with the initial ten. Once they get those down, I introduce knees, elbows, side kicks, and turning side kicks. The turning side kick is the last one I teach since turning full circle adds an element of risk.

When it comes to fighting on your feet, you can never forget about movement and footwork. I have often said that footwork and movement are more important than the actual strikes. Perfect striking technique does not matter if you cannot get into the right position to use it. If you are using perfect punching and kicking techniques but are doing so at the wrong distance or the wrong time or are hitting the wrong areas, it does you no good. On the same note, if you use bad form but use it at the right distance at the right time, hitting the right spots, though your technique may be poor, you can still be dangerous.

Think of it like this: it does not take a lot of power or pressure to finish a fight with an accurate body shot to the ribs or strike to the chin. What matters is the amount of force required to finish a fight. If you throw a punch, and your opponent sees it coming and blocks it with their hand, it will take a ton of force to transfer the energy from your fist through their hand and knock them out. Even if you are using perfect technique, you will likely not be able to create enough energy transfer from your fist through their hand and secure a knockout victory.

Now, let's look at the amount of energy required to secure a knockout win when it is a clean, unblocked shot taken on the chin. I would love to give you a number on the pressure per square inch required to knock someone out, but too many variables affect that number. I have knocked people out and dropped people with body shots I didn't think had enough power or energy to be effective. But these punches caused enough damage to stop the fight because I hit them in the right spot. I have done this both in sanctioned fights and accidentally while sparring with friends. It does not take a lot of force to deliver a fight-winning blow.

The important thing is making contact in the right areas and it's footwork that puts you in the right area at the right time. Once you expose your opponent's vulnerable areas using footwork and movement, it's just a matter of reaching out and hitting them where it counts. If you have seen many knockouts, one thing you will often notice is that people use all kinds of crazy, ugly techniques. But when that crazy, ugly technique hits a vulnerable area, you've got a fight-winning blow. People have asked me what is more important: perfect striking technique or footwork and movement. My answer is footwork and movement—but don't let that be an excuse for sloppy striking technique.

As a fighter, you must constantly work on footwork and movement. Beyond that, you should always be working on mixing perfect striking technique with great footwork and movement. When you create an opportunity to win using footwork and movement, you want to hit your opponent's vulnerable areas with maximum power using perfect striking technique. That should be your goal: perfect striking technique mixed with great footwork and movement.

Good footwork and movement also promote good defense. Let's look at footwork and movement principles and see how they support defensive techniques. The techniques I will cover are stance, steps, step back counter, pivot, slips, rolls, ducks, and lean.

Stance

If you are right-handed, put your left foot forward; it will be your lead foot. If you are left-handed, put your right foot forward; it will be your lead foot. With one foot forward at a comfortable distance (about shoulder-width apart), point your lead foot toward your opponent. Your rear foot angles out about forty-five degrees off your lead foot. Now that you have the right footing, you need the right stance. The right stance is high on your toes with a slight bend in your knees, hands held high to protect your face, and elbows in tight to protect your body. Once you get the stance down, you can move on to steps.

Steps

Every technique in fighting should be a controlled motion practiced thousands of times, even the way you step. It's not complicated, but it can be difficult to execute properly during a fight, when nerves are strained. Repetition is key. Many coaches, including myself, use footwork drills to warm fighters up before practice. The most basic thing about footwork is never letting your feet get close together, especially never crossing your feet as you are stepping around. If you move forward, put your lead foot forward first. Your stance will become wide for a moment, but then your back foot will step up and you will regain your original footing. You need to follow your lead foot forward and your rear foot backward. Your left foot will step first if going left, your right foot first when going right. Doing this keeps your stance wide and helps you avoid a narrow stance or accidentally crossing your feet.

Step Back Counter

Once you can step properly, you're ready for one of the most important moves in fighting: the step back. The step back is not just a defensive move, it's a defensive and offensive move at the same time. It's defensive because usually I step back to avoid getting hit. Once you avoid the strike with a step back, you need to regain your ground and counter with a combo. Step back counter works well because when someone attempts a strike and completely misses, they often expose themselves, and this counterstrike becomes a great tool. It's a quick step back counterstrike.

Pivot

The basics of the pivot step are to be high on your toes, dig the ball of one foot into the ground, and make a step, pushing off the other foot and rotating a new angle—about ninety degrees. The most common pivot step for a right-handed person is to take the lead left foot and dig the ball of that foot into the ground. The lead left foot becomes the pivot foot that stays in place as you rotate ninety degrees, and it's the back foot you push off to create the new angle. Pivoting can also be defensive and offensive. I like to use the pivot step when someone is rushing me. Rather than backing up to avoid the strikes, the pivot can quickly move you out of the way so you can set up counterstrikes.

Now that we have talked about basic footwork, let's look at another kind of movement: slips, rolls, duck, and lean. This type of movement is used to dodge strikes. Moving with steps is good, but it's different than the movement we're talking about here, which consists of moving your body with your knees and rolling your feet back and forth to move your head while you are holding your ground.

Slips

A simple way to slip a punch is to push off your feet. It's not a push that creates a step but a push that creates movement. Your left foot will rotate, turning your heel up. As your foot rotates and turns your heel up, it will push your head the opposite direction just a few inches—just enough to avoid the strike. If you are right-handed, a lead left foot rotation while lifting your heel will push your head to the right a few inches. A rear right foot rotation and heel lift will push your head to the left a few inches—just enough to keep your head moving to avoid any major strikes to your chin.

I often say less is more when it comes to defense. Your slip movement needs to be a small and fast, back and forth, left to right. Making a big slip to your right can double the amount of time it takes to turn your body back to the left. It should be a short, quick movement just a few inches to one side and then another short, quick movement back to the other side a few inches. Making a big slip can offset your stance and cause you to miss a counter opportunity or become unable to move into your next defensive strategy. I often see fighters move to one side and get stuck on that side. A common problem for a right-handed fighter is they will make a big defensive movement to the right and get stuck on that side; what starts as a simple slip to the right leads to being bent over to the right and getting pushed into the ropes, or cage, which is never a good thing. Remember to keep your defense fast and simple.

Rolls

Rolls are similar to slipping left to right, pushing off your feet, and lifting your heel. But for a roll, you use your knees to drop your elevation. Now you are not just moving side to side but also up and down. Rolls enable you to drop your head under an opponent's hook and come up on the other side. If a right-handed person slips to his left, he can then roll back to his right. If you find yourself off to the left of your stance, you drop your level by bending your knees, rotating your feet, then standing up on the right side of your stance. What happens is your feet and knees work together to take your head from one side of your stance so you can drop your level and pop up on the other side of your stance. As with the slips, speed is key. Making your rolls big and slow can become counterproductive. Your rolls also need to be sharp and quick.

Duck

A duck is used to avoid a strike. As simple as it is, I see many fighters get it wrong. The most common mistake is when people bend over at the waist as they duck. Doing so takes your eyes off your opponent and throws your stance off-center. The right way to duck is to keep your eyes on your opponent and use your knees to drop your level straight down and then come straight up. The difference between a duck and a roll is that a roll starts on one side of your stance, drops your level, rotates, and picks you up on the other side. A duck is a quick straight down and straight up. Like the roll, it's quick and has just enough movement to avoid the strike.

Lean

A lean is a simple move many pick up naturally. If someone tries to punch you in the face, you naturally lean back to avoid being hit. Where people go wrong is they lean from a flat-footed stance. If you are standing flat-footed, you will lean back at your waist. This puts all your weight on your heels. Your toes then come up off the ground and compromise your stance, weaken your counterstrikes, and restrict your ability to make your next defensive movement. The key to a good lean is to be high on your toes with your heel off the mat. When you are high on your toes, you can lean by lowering your rear heel an inch or two. Lowering your rear heel an inch or two moves your face back five or six inches. If your rear heel is always three inches up, you can now drop it one or two inches and still not be flat-footed. By dropping your back foot two inches, you can move your head back five inches and not be flat-footed. With a proper lean, you can still slip, roll, or counterstrike with a lot of power. The other common mistake fighters make as they lean is they stretch their hand away from their face. As you lean, you still need your hands up near your face; then, if an unexpected strike comes, your hands are up and ready to block.

That was a quick overview of the footwork and movements critical during a fight. Remember, your first line of defense is footwork and movement.

Now the second type of defense I would like to cover consists of blocking techniques: catch, parry, cover, and checking.

Catch

This is when someone tries to punch you and you catch the punch, just as you would catch a baseball, with your palm open. While catching a strike, you should catch with very little movement. If you catch with big movement, such as lunging and stretching to catch, it may stop the punch, but it draws your hands away from your face and leaves you open for a second or third punch. A small catch right in front of your face is more effective than a big catch away from your face.

The other advice I always give while teaching the catch technique is to catch on the same side. If you and your opponent face off, your opposite hands line up. As you stand face-to-face, your right hand is straight across from his left hand, his right straight across from your left. A catch should be carried out on the same side as the strike. A right straight should be caught with a left catch and vice versa. Catching on the same side keeps your hands in a good defensive position. Catching on the opposite side puts both your hands on the same side of your face, leaving one side exposed.

Parry

A parry is similar to a catch, but while a catch stops the punch, a parry deflects it. If a punch is coming straight at your face, you can often just turn your wrist slightly. That little wrist movement will make contact with the punch and deflect it from striking your face. Just like the catch, it needs to be a small movement. That way, after the parry, you can quickly bring your hand back up to your face. As with the catch, it needs to stay on the same side so you don't cross your hands and leave one side of your face exposed.

Cover

People often call the cover technique "answer the phone" because that's what it looks like as you put your fist up to your ear. You can cover on one side to block one punch, or you can lift both hands to your ears and face and do a complete cover. A complete cover can block multiple punches because it covers most of your face. But one problem with the complete cover is that it does not cover all of your face and body. As you raise both fists to your ears, you also need to tuck your chin in and keep your elbows tight to your body to protect your ribs. But even if you do it right, you can't protect everything—there will always be something exposed. If you sit in a complete cover long enough, it's only a matter of time before your opponent finds your vulnerable area and attacks it. When it comes to the cover defense, I like to quickly cover one side of my face to block one punch, then move or block using a different technique or counterstrike. I will use the complete cover when necessary, but many times when fighters use the complete cover, it's because they get lazy. Covering also restricts sight and movement, and that is never a good thing in fighting. Remember, when covering, make it quick, then go to your next move.

Checking

Checking is fairly easy to learn. When you are in a good fight stance, high on your toes, and someone tries to kick your legs, you can check their kick. As they kick you, you lift your knee and turn your shin toward the oncoming kick. One thing I like to do when I see the kick coming is keep the check leg stiff and slightly push into the check with my hips so I'm not just raising a check. In a way, I'm attacking his kick so it hurts the kicker when it lands shin to shin in hopes of preventing him from using that kick again. I like to use three different checks. The main difference in the three is the level to which I raise the check. For a low check, I lift my foot about six inches off the ground. For the mid check, I lift my foot about twelve inches. For a high check, I raise my knee to my elbow. Having your knee to your elbow and your hand at your face creates a solid defense from your hand down to your knee and your knee all the way down to your foot. Doing a high check usually brings my foot about twenty-four inches off the ground.

That covers the basic defensive moves and blocks one must master to be a good stand-up fighter. With practice, these basic principles should flow together as one. As you are stepping, you should be mixing in movements, and as you are stepping and moving, you should have your hands up and showing different blocks, even if your opponent is not throwing any punches. You can frustrate your opponent simply by constantly showing different steps, movements, blocks, and covers.

Wrestling

Wrestling is the art of takedowns and takedown defense.

One way to think of a takedown is to grab and anchor on one part of your opponent's body. With your anchor in place, you try to get them off balance by pushing, pulling, lifting, spinning, circling, or tripping. So what do you grab? What is the anchor? I've come up with a system that helps me keep my mind open to all possibilities. While wrestling, you should be looking to take someone down on nine different parts of their body, also referred to as levels:

- Ankles
- Knee or knees
- Hips
- Chest and shoulders
- Grabbing their arm and going under it
- Grabbing their arm and going over it
- Neck
- Pushing their head straight back
- Pulling their head down

At *level one* we attack the ankle. We can call this attack an ankle pick, but there are many types of ankle picks. Which ankle pick you use doesn't matter much. If the ankle is available, attack it, and use the ankle to get a takedown.

Level two is the knees. There are many ways to take your opponent down at the knee level. The most common is the single-leg or double-leg takedown. Even still there are many different types of single- and double-leg takedowns. Don't overthink it. If you can get your arms and hands locked around your opponent's legs, do it; lower your level, and shoot for your opponent's legs.

Level three is the hips. Similar to attacking your opponent's legs, you drop and shoot at the hip level so you can lock your hands around their hips. Locking your hands around their hips is a great anchor point. As you pull their hips in, pick their hips up, push, pull, then look for a trip or use the hip lock to maneuver behind them for a rear takedown. Locking your arms and hands around your opponent's hips can give you a great takedown advantage.

Level four is when you anchor on your opponent's chest and shoulders. A common position in fighting and grappling is a tie-up, where you have several anchor points available. One is where you lock your hands around your opponent's chest and one of their arms, then turn and throw toward their trapped arm. The other is where you lock your hands around just their body and chest area with the goal to work it down to their hips, or if they lock around your body, you can overlock around both their arms to break their grip or throw with that overarm lock. If you can't lock your hands around your opponent, just grip one of his arms tightly on the triceps shoulder area and then with the other arm hook under his armpit and look for throws and trips.

Level five is getting behind your opponent by going under his arm. Wrestlers have a common move called a "duck under," which is basically ducking your head under their arm to get behind them. There are many variations of the duck under. Some push their opponent's elbow up and duck under as the elbow is up in the air. Others grab their opponent's wrist and lift their whole arm up. It doesn't really matter how you get the arm up; all that matters is that when the arm goes up, you cut under it and get behind them. You want to get behind them because when you are behind someone with your arms and hands locked around them, it gives you a huge advantage and makes it easy to take them down with trips and throws.

Level six is going over their arm to get behind them and take their back. It's a lot like level five, where you go under their arm to take their back, but level six goes over the arm using a technique called an arm drag. When I do an arm drag, I like to grab their wrist on the same side, cross grab under their armpit, then hook on the back side of their shoulder. When I pull that shoulder, I step toward my opponent, moving his body toward me as I step toward him and around his arm to get behind him. Once again, there are many ways to drag an arm to take someone's back. The important thing is that when given the chance to drag over an arm, we do it so we can take advantage of all the opportunities of being behind someone.

Level seven is using your opponent's head and neck as an anchor point. A common head and neck takedown is a head throw, which is where you grab their triceps with one hand and wrap your other arm around their neck as you twist and throw. It's their head that gets tugged on, and they get spun around and thrown to their back. The head throw is a good head and neck takedown.

Level eight is more of a setup move, but it works so well I gave it its own number. It's simple. You just push their head back or side to side, exposing their entire body from the ankle to the neck. If there is not an immediate move available, give their head a good push, and see what opens up. It always works.

Level nine is along the same lines as level eight and is also a setup move. But rather than pushing your opponent's head, you're pulling it down. Simply take one hand, grab the back of their neck, and pull their head down. Most people won't let you pull their neck and head down. As they resist and look up, they often stand up as well. That is an example of how pulling their head down sets up a takedown. As they resist and go up, you lunge or shoot under to grab their legs, ankles, hips, or whatever you can to get the takedown. It's mostly a setup move because all you're doing is pulling their head down, but with some aggression and a quick snap, you can use it as a takedown. As your opponent stumbles, you can quickly swing around to their back.

Along with the offensive side of wrestling, there is also the defensive side. Often, stopping a takedown will give you a takedown, and training in takedown defense is just as important as training in takedown offense.

Let's talk about the progression of takedown defense. It starts with a good stance. When your opponent goes for a takedown, step out of their way. If that's not enough, sprawl; if they're still attacking, cross face. I've listed it as if it's something I do step-by-step, one move at a time. But over time as you practice each move, you can start putting different moves together to where it becomes as if they were one solid movement.

A good stance will put you in position to dodge and defend. It can also make your opponent hesitate and not even want to go for a takedown, because getting a takedown against someone with a good stance is difficult. If you're in an MMA fight, you should always use a good fight stance—high hands, bent knees, standing tall, chin down, feet shoulder width apart, one dominant lead foot, on your toes, your feet always moving.

If you're grappling, your feet will be a bit wider than shoulder width. You'll sink into a low squatting stance, stay on your toes, and move your feet while your hands and elbows are tight to your body—some call it T-rex arms.

We have both a fight stance and a grappling stance because if you use a wrestling stance in an MMA fight, you will get punched or kicked in the head. The grappling stance leaves you vulnerable to strikes. It also limits the power in your strikes and what strikes you can do.

But in a grappling match, where takedowns and takedown defense is the name of the game, you need a low center of gravity to keep your opponent from getting under you. A low center of gravity allows you to get under them instead. Keep your hands and arms tight against your body in a grappling match so you can defend yourself against their takedown attacks.

So, first, get your stance. Second, step out of their way. A quick side step always leaves you in a good position. You can step back, but stepping back often leaves you with your back against the wall. If you do step back, your next step needs to be a side step.

Your third move is to sprawl. I sprawl when they grab my leg, then drop all my weight on top of them, kick my legs back, keeping them straight and wide. I also stay on my toes with all my weight on their shoulder, neck, and head area.

Your fourth move is to do a cross face. I use a cross face when my opponent has grabbed my leg so tight a sprawl is not enough to avoid the takedown. When my opponent is low under my hips and has a tight grip around one or both of my legs, I will reach down and put the bony part of my wrist against their nose. The bony part of the wrist is the part right behind your thumb and is called the radius. Once I place my radius on the bridge of their nose, I crank it in a quick, violent rip. If done right, you can get anyone to let go, I don't care how strong they are. If they hold tight, you can easily break their nose. If they are stubborn and don't care if their nose is broken, keep ripping and cranking. If you torque your wrist across their face, you can crank their neck around with your hips and legs. Once their neck gets cranked around, they can't hold on to your leg anymore. No one can. I don't care how strong or stubborn someone is, once you feel your neck might break, your body will let go, and there is nothing you can do about it.

Those are my four favorite defensive takedown movements: stance, side steps, sprawl, and cross face. All are done in one fluid movement. If done right, often you will only need to use a good stance and steps. But if that's not enough, punish them with a sprawl and cross face.

Jiu-Jitsu

It's my belief that jiu-jitsu, or submission grappling, is the most complicated and difficult martial art to learn. To help you fully understand it, I'll break jiu-jitsu down into nine different positions. All nine positions have a top side and a bottom side, which means we now have eighteen different positions—nine top, and nine bottom. How I list it at the gym is:

Top		Bottom
1	Stand up	2
3	Front headlock	4
5	Guard	6
7	Half guard	8
9	Side control	10
11	Side sit	12
13	Mount	14
15	Rear	16
17	North south	18

This is the jiu-jitsu structure I personally use and the format I use to teach grappling. For each area of jiu-jitsu —all the positions on top and all the positions on bottom—I require my athletes to memorize three different goals. With eighteen areas and three goals for each area, that gives you fifty-four different moves, or goals. The reason I don't just call them fifty-four moves is because the first thing you should go for is the position within the position. The first goal should always be to get the best position possible within that position. For example, in side control bottom (number ten on the chart above), you would be lying underneath your opponent. But lying flat on your back is not a proper position for bottom side control; you should never be lying underneath someone in a fight. When you are in bottom side control, your first goal should be to turn into your opponent, shrimp your hips away, and sit up. As you sit up and turn into your opponent, put one elbow on the mat and one side of your hips into the mat. You will be free to use your arm for an under hook and your legs and feet to scoot out and around to get behind your opponent.

I'm not going to go into all the possible moves in each position because that would be a book in and of itself. Jiu-jitsu is complicated, but I hope this guide helps you categorize and structure a number of different movements.

Ground and Pound

Ground and pound is fairly easy to learn but is often overlooked. And it's an area in which I see fighters make a lot of mistakes. While striking someone on the ground, you have many different strikes to choose from that are similar to the strikes used in stand-up fighting. You can punch straight down. A straight-down punch is similar to a one-two in a stand-up fight. Basically, when you are on your knees and over the top of someone, you just throw jabs and crosses straight down at them. You can also hook your punches like in a stand-up fight, otherwise known as a three-four. A three-four in a ground and pound is used to hook your punches around their blocks to make contact. You can also uppercut like a five and six.

There are a few more strikes that aren't necessarily punches but still work well. A hammer fist is a lot like a karate chop but with a closed fist that strikes with the side of your hand. And, of course, there are knees. In US-sanctioned MMA fights, knees to the head of a *grounded opponent* is illegal, but you can throw knees to the body all you want. Lastly, there are elbows—my favorite ground-and-pound technique, though it is illegal for an amateur fighter in Utah to throw an elbow. In most sanctioned fights, elbows are mostly for pro fighters, depending on the athletic commission they are fighting for. Constantly changing the angles of your strikes makes you dangerous while on top of someone. Here is a full list of the ground-and-pound strikes I mentioned:

- Straights, or one-two
- Hooks, or three-four
- Uppercuts, or five-six
- Hammer fist
- Knees to the body
- Elbows (for the pros)

If you can keep all of these strikes at the forefront of your mind, you will be a more effective fighter. But in the heat of the moment, it's hard to think clearly and remember all the strikes available to you. I see many fighters in ground-and-pound situations attacking the head even if their opponent is blocking their head. At these times I use a phrase to remind myself to find all the different striking opportunities—"two to one," which means hit them in one area twice, then once in another area, and then repeat over and over until the referee pulls you off. There is no exact formula. For example, it could be two straight punches and one elbow, or two knees and one hammer fist. The list goes on and on. The combinations and strikes can be mixed however you want. The beauty of the two-to-one combo is that, often, as you hit one part of the body twice, your opponent will move their defense to the part of the body you are attacking. Then, when you see their body and defense shift, you can hit a new area with a different strike. Just keep your eyes peeled so you can see the next available striking opportunity.

Mixing Arts

Mixing arts is the last of all the arts because you can't start mixing until you have a solid foundation in each individual art. You must practice until you have rid yourself of all your bad habits and developed good habits. With a good understanding of fighting technique basics, new habits developed, and old habits lost, you can start mixing techniques.

Every fight starts in the standing position. My favorite strikes to get the fight going are boxing combos using straight punches—just a series of ones and twos. Most the time I don't even try to hit my opponent with any of my first combos. As I'm throwing my combos at the air, I focus on footwork and movement. Often the opponent will rush in and start the action. If they are patient and don't do much, I start the action after about ten or fifteen seconds. The first combo I often use is a boxing combo finished with a kick, also known as a Muay Thai combo. I really like the boxing-to-kicking technique. For the most part, stand-up fighting is a series of punches that leads to kicks, knees, or elbows, depending on how your opponent moves or defends. Just as I use punches to set up kicks, knees, and elbows, punches should also be used to set up takedowns. A fast, aggressive boxing combo is a great setup for a takedown. If you can occupy your opponent with striking defense, they will forget about takedown defense, which allows you to score an effortless takedown.

Once I get on top of someone, I use a technique called "strike to sub and sub to strike," which means you let your strikes set up submissions and let your submissions set up strikes. On one hand, while I'm striking a grounded opponent, I look at their arms and neck to see if there are any submissions available. On the other, while I'm attempting submissions, I'm looking for strikes to their face or body. If I'm struggling to get the submission, it's often better just to let go of whatever I'm holding on to and to start striking. And if none of the strikes are landing, I go back to looking for a submission.

No one can defend everything all the time; everyone has an opening and opportunity for moves and strikes somewhere. Just stay active to make sure you win the judges' scorecard, and if things go your way, you will get a knockout, technical knockout, or submission win. And if not a finish victory, make sure you are always punching to set up kicks, knees, elbows, and takedowns. Then, once you are on the ground, "strike to sub and sub to strike." If you are constantly using these techniques, even if you don't finish with a knockout or submission, there is a good chance you will win the fight based on the judges' scorecards.

Fighting has many more techniques, principles, positions, and moves. This was just a quick overview of some of the most basic fighting fundamentals, but it illustrates how complex fighting is and how, if your goal is to become a great fighter, you must spend time learning each art and structure the sport of fighting in a way that makes it easier to learn. It's vital to have a team and coach that help you get moving in the right direction, but no matter how hard you train with your team and coach, when it comes time to fight, it's just you and you alone, and having a structure and goals is key to your success.

About the Author

ERIC WAHLIN, CO-OWNER OF FACTUM MMA, has been competing in combat sports most of his life. He has won many different titles, including a high school state wrestling championship, a freestyle state wrestling championship, and the North American Grappling Association championship ten times, all of which were in the black-belt gi and expert no-gi divisions. Wahlin has an undefeated professional heavyweight boxing record of 3-0. In MMA he has won and defended Utah's Steelfist light-heavyweight title and has fought in Bellator and the Ultimate Fighter. In the LDS Church, he served for two years as a missionary in the Washington, DC South area. He has continued to serve in a variety of callings and is now a Sunday School teacher. In *Fighting to Find God* he takes all of his experiences as a professional fighter and applies them to the spiritual search everyone must go through to attain a relationship with God.

Note to the Reader

THANK YOU FOR TAKING THE time to read my book. If you find that my message was inspiring and helpful, please recommend it to your friends and family as I feel everyone can benefit from building a relationship with God. It would be much appreciated if you also left a review on Amazon.

Made in the USA
San Bernardino, CA
17 February 2019